GEOGRAPHY

EARTH 2

Earth & Its Neighbors

HERON BOOKS

At Heron Books, we think learning should be engaging and fun. It should be hands-on and it should allow students to move at their own pace.

For this purpose, we have created an accompanying learning guide to help the student progress through this book, chapter by chapter, with increasing confidence, interest and independence.

Get your free learning guide at
heronbooks.com/learningguides.

For a final exam, email
teacherresources@heronbooks.com.

We would love to hear from you!
Email us at *feedback@heronbooks.com*.

Published by
Heron Books, Inc.
20950 SW Rock Creek Road
Sheridan, OR 97378

heronbooks.com

Special thanks to all the teachers and students who
provided feedback instrumental to this edition.

Fifth Edition © 1977, 2019, Heron Books
All Rights Reserved

ISBN: 0-89739-041-5

Any unauthorized copying, translation, duplication or distribution, in whole or in part, by any means, including electronic copying, storage or transmission, is a violation of applicable laws.

Printed in the USA

10 June 2019

IN THIS BOOK

1 THE EARTH 1

2 DAYS AND NIGHTS 15
    Activity Days and Nights.................................... 27

3 YEARS 29
    Activity Earth Rotates and Revolves 35

4 THE MOON 37

5 DISTANCES IN SPACE 47
    Activity Distances in Space 52

6 HOW EARTH TURNS 55
    Activity Earth's Axis Is Tilted............................ 61

7 SEASONS 63
    Activity What Causes the Seasons?................. 74

8 THE WAY THE MOON LOOKS 77

9 WHY THE MOON SEEMS TO CHANGE........... 83
    Activity Why the Moon Seems to Change 89

10 ORBITS AND PLANETS....................................... 93

11 THE SOLAR SYSTEM 99

12 ASTEROIDS AND FALLING STARS 107

13 COMETS 113

1
The Earth

THE EARTH

LOOKING AT THE EARTH

When we go outside we can see ground and houses and trees.

THE EARTH

As we move away from the trees and houses, they look smaller.

The farther we go away from them, the smaller they look.

If we went up in an airplane high above the ground, the trees and houses would look even smaller.

THE EARTH

If we went way, way up and looked down, we wouldn't be able to see the houses and trees at all. We would see something that looks like a huge ball. We would see lots of water and big pieces of land. Sometimes we would see clouds over the water and land. This big round ball is called **Earth**.

If we went even farther away, Earth would look like a smaller ball.

A huge ball in space like this is called a **planet**. Some people like to call Earth "planet Earth."

THE EARTH

Earth is made out of rocks and dirt and water, and has air around it.

Earth does not look round when we are standing on it because it is so very big and we are so close to it.

THE EARTH

GLOBES

When we study about Earth, we sometimes use a globe. A **globe** is a model of planet Earth.

On a globe, the oceans are usually colored blue and the land is a different color. You can often find things out about Earth by looking at a globe.

THE EARTH

PEOPLE LIVE ALL OVER EARTH

Many people live on this planet with us. People live almost everywhere on the planet where there is land.

Of course, the people are really much smaller on the planet than they look in this drawing.

THE EARTH

THE EARTH

People live all around the planet. Because our planet is like a ball, it looks like some of the people could fall off. But they don't, because our planet pulls everything on it toward the center or middle of the planet. This pull is called **gravity**. You can see gravity at work when you drop something and it falls to the ground. Gravity holds things on the planet.

Gravity pulls you toward the planet, and that direction is always called **down**. The other direction (away from the planet) is called **up**. So anywhere you go on Earth the sky is up and the ground under your feet is down.

When you look at a globe or a picture of the planet, it looks like some of the people would be upside down. But, if you went to the places where those people are, it would not seem like you were upside down. When you looked up, you would still see the sky. When you looked down, you would see the ground.

THE EARTH

LAND, WATER AND AIR

On planet Earth there are big areas of land called **continents**. Most of the people on Earth live on the continents. Some live on islands.

The earth also has big areas of water. These are called **oceans**.

There is air around our planet. The blanket of air around Earth is called the **atmosphere** (AT-mos-fear). Our bodies need this air to live. We breathe it all the time.

THE SUN

The **sun** is a huge, burning ball that we see in the sky during the day. The light from the sun shines on Earth and gives us light and heat. We can feel the heat from the sun when we go outside on a sunny day. The light and heat from the sun make it possible for living things to grow on Earth.

The sun is much bigger than Earth. It is very far away, much farther than it looks in this picture.

2

Days and Nights

DAYS AND NIGHTS

One meaning of **day** is the time it is light outside.

These boys are playing outside during the day.

Night is the time it is dark outside.

THE EARTH SPINS

Day and night happen because the earth spins.

To us it feels like Earth is standing still, but it is really turning around and around. It turns all the way around in 24 hours. Another word for spinning or turning is **rotate**. So we say that the earth **rotates** because it spins around. You can show this with a globe.

DAYS AND NIGHTS

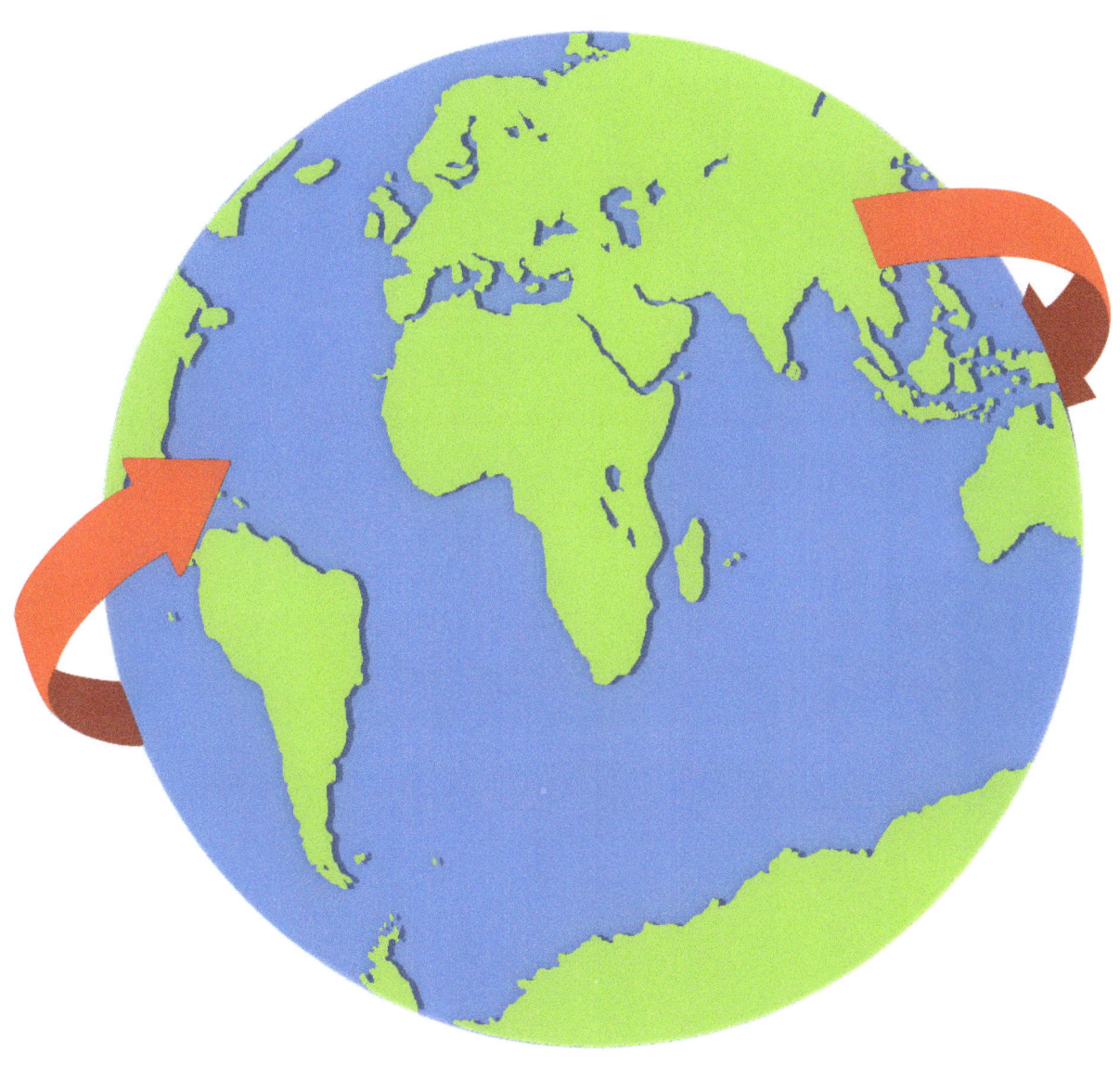

DAYS AND NIGHTS

THE SPINNING EARTH MAKES DAY AND NIGHT

As Earth rotates, the sun shines on one side of the planet so it is light on that side. It is day there. The side of the planet that is turned away from the sun is dark. It is night there.

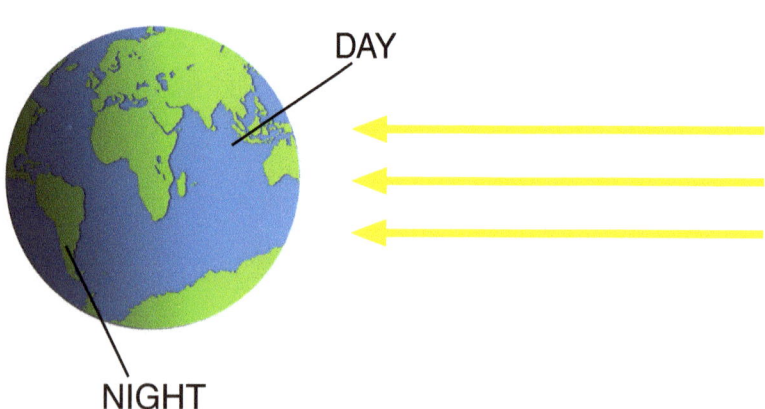

DAYS AND NIGHTS

Suppose this is you standing on Earth in the dark. It is night for you.

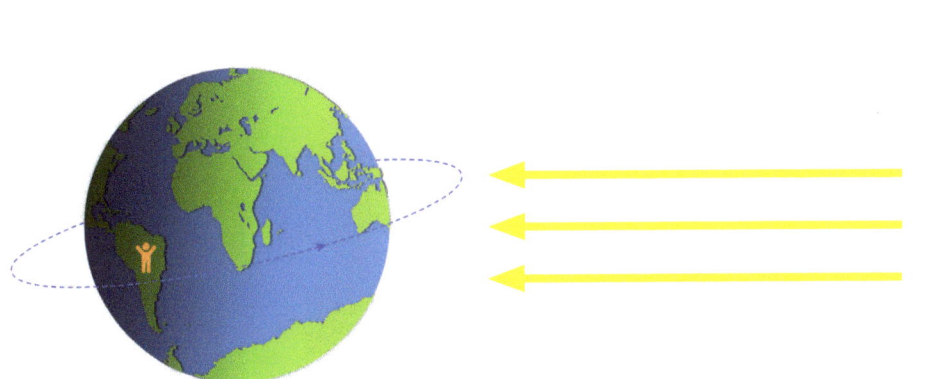

DAYS AND NIGHTS

Earth continues to turn and soon you are in the light—now it is day for you.

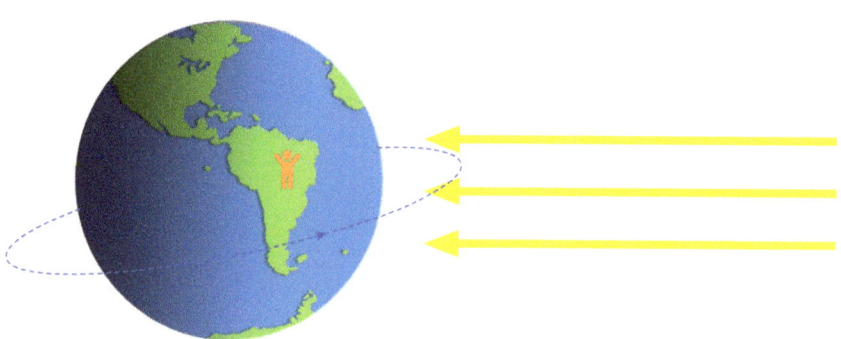

DAYS AND NIGHTS

Earth continues to rotate, so night turns to day and day turns to night, again and again. Each time Earth makes a complete turn all the way through night and day is called a complete rotation.

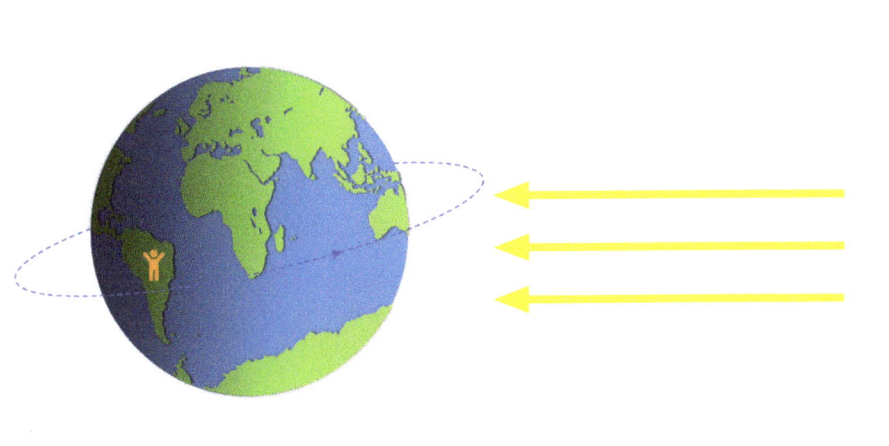

DAYS AND NIGHTS

This is another meaning of **day**—the time it takes Earth to make one complete turn or rotation. So, day can mean "the time it is light," or "the time it takes the earth to spin all the way around once."

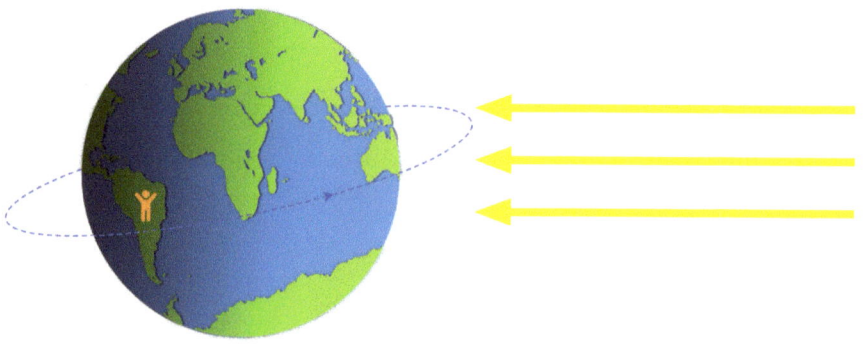

If the earth didn't rotate, we would not have day and night. It would just stay dark on one side all the time and light on the other.

DAYS AND NIGHTS

THE SUN COMES UP AND GOES DOWN

You may have heard someone say that the sun comes up in the morning and goes down in the evening. Actually, the sun doesn't move. It only seems to move because of the turning of the earth.

Suppose it is morning where you are and there is just starting to be light. If you face in the direction of the sun, you will see the sun seem to come up just a bit and then rise higher and higher in the sky. The sun *looks* like it is rising up because Earth is rotating toward the sun.

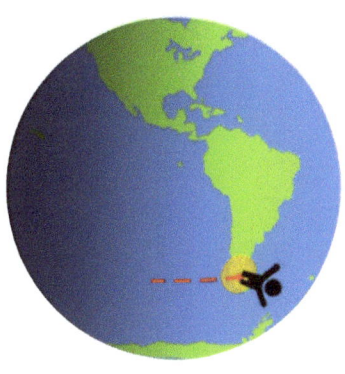

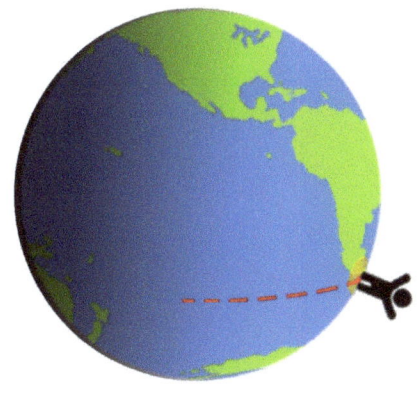

The turning of Earth makes it look like the sun keeps getting higher and higher until noon. At noon the sun is high overhead.

DAYS AND NIGHTS

Earth continues to turn and in the afternoon it looks like the sun is sinking. It gets lower and lower until you can't see it anymore.

When the sun goes down in the evening, it goes down in the opposite direction from where it came up.

If you face the direction where the sun came up, you will see that the sun goes down behind you.

Activity
Days and Nights

For this activity, you will need a globe, a small piece of clay and a small lamp without a shade.

- ☐ Get a globe, and find where you live. Put a small blob of clay there to mark the spot. If you want to, you can make the clay look like a tiny person.

- ☐ Place the globe and a small lamp without a shade on a table or on the floor. They should be several feet apart.

- ☐ Turn on the lamp and turn off the lights in the room. Rotate the globe so the blob of clay is on the side where the light is shining. It is day there.

- ☐ Now slowly rotate the globe to the right until the clay blob moves into the dark. Now it is night.

- ☐ Keep rotating the globe to the right until the clay blob comes back into the light. Can you see how a person standing there might think the sun was rising higher and higher in the sky?

- ☐ Keep rotating the globe in the same direction until the clay blob is out of the light and it is night. To a person standing there it would look like the sun is going down, but they are really just moving away from the sun.

3 Years

YEARS

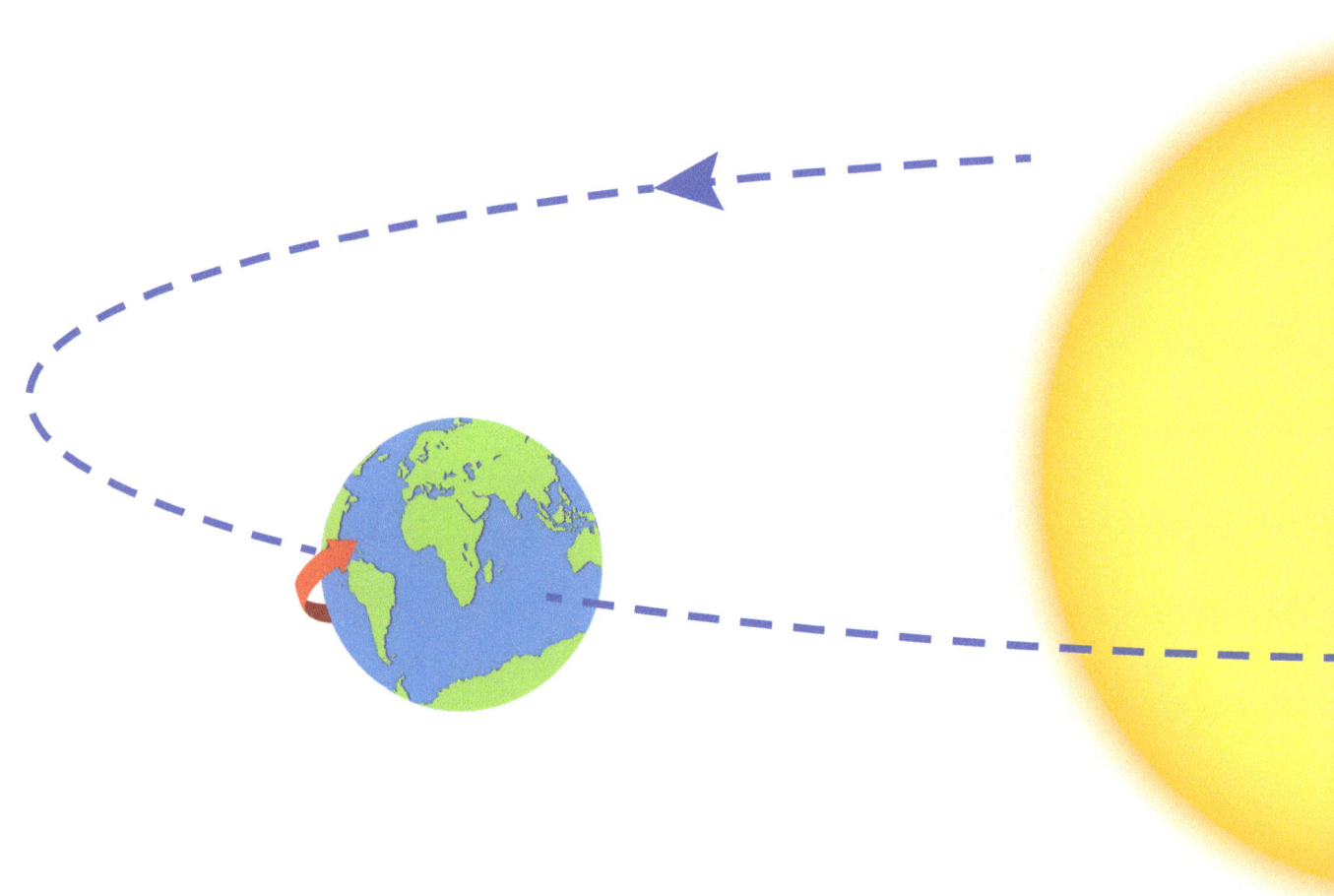

While Earth is rotating through day and night, it is also moving around the sun. It moves around the sun in a big circle.

When we talk about Earth turning through day and night, we say it is rotating. When we talk about Earth moving around the sun, we say it is revolving. **Revolving** means "to be moving in a circle."

Earth takes a long time to move all the way around the sun. We call the amount of time Earth takes to move all the way around the sun a **year**.

YEARS

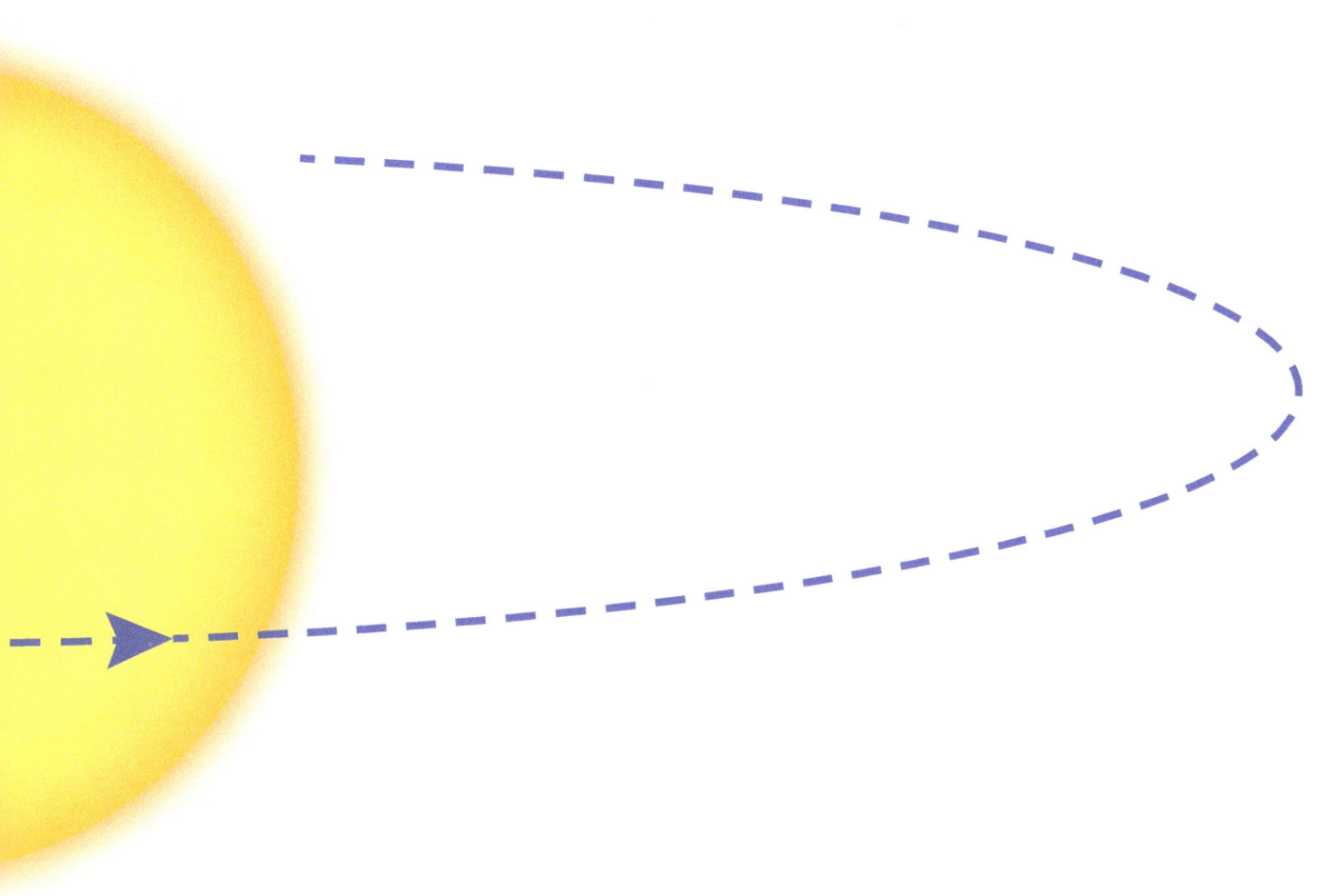

From the day you were born until your first birthday, Earth revolved all the way around the sun and one year went by. So on your first birthday, we said you were "one year old." One more year went by before your next birthday. Then we said you were "two years old."

From one birthday to the next birthday, one year always goes by. That means that between your birthdays Earth has revolved once, or made one whole trip around the sun.

YEARS

Suppose your birthday happened when the earth was here.

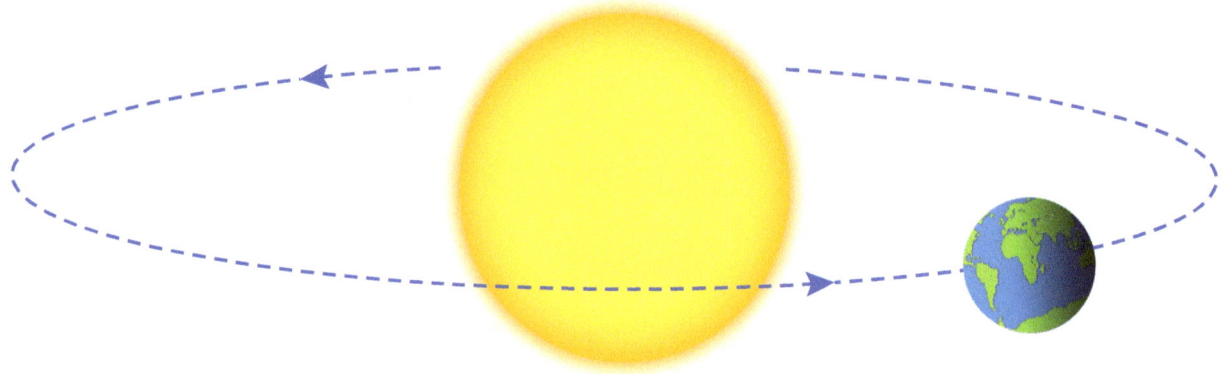

Then part of the year later, the earth would be here.

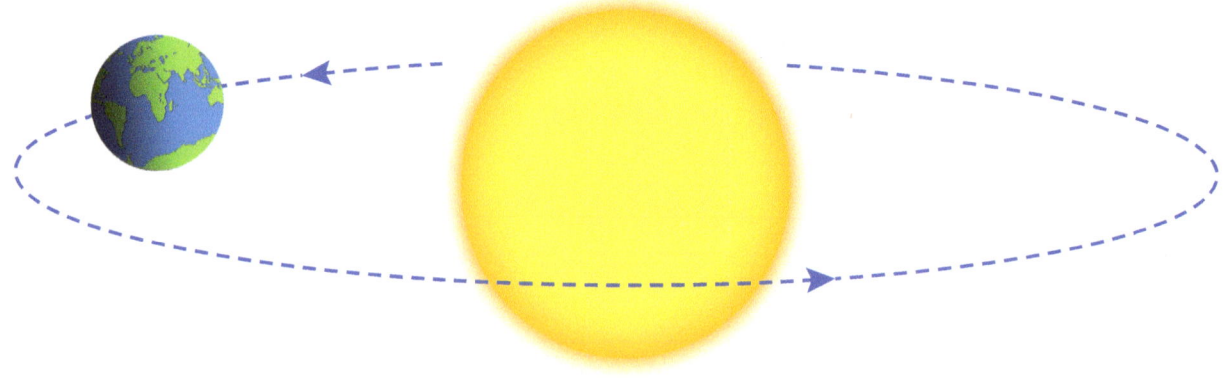

YEARS

Then when it was your birthday again, the earth would have moved back here.

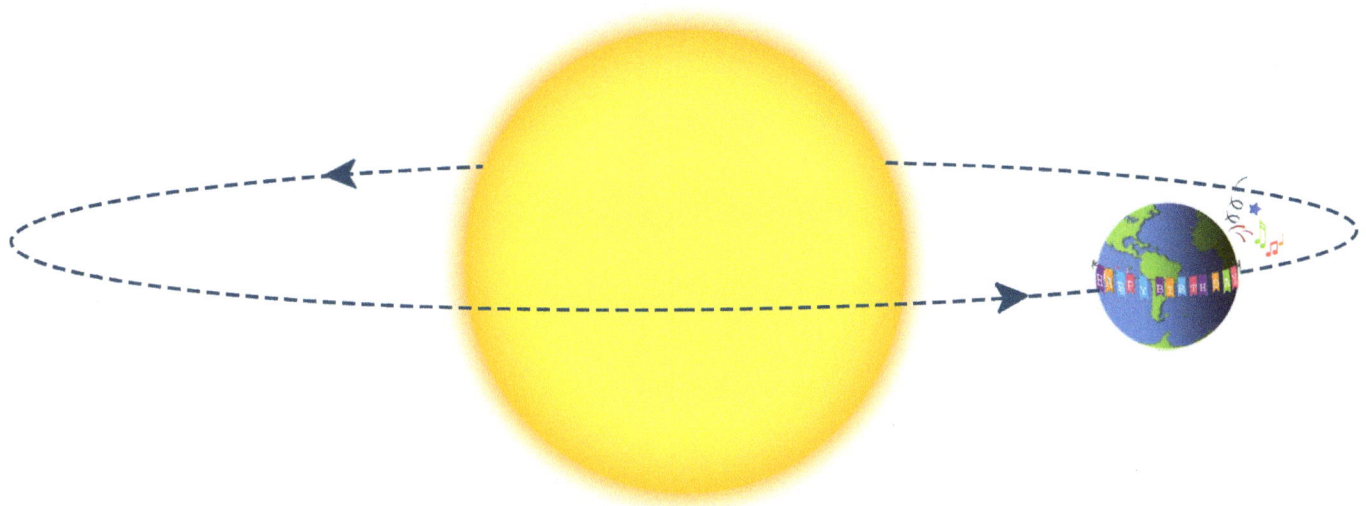

Earth has made one trip around the sun and one year has gone by.

YEARS

EARTH REVOLVES AND ROTATES AT THE SAME TIME

So, Earth moves in two ways. It moves in a circle around the sun, or revolves. It also spins, or rotates.

Earth makes just one trip around the sun each year, but it makes a complete rotation every day.

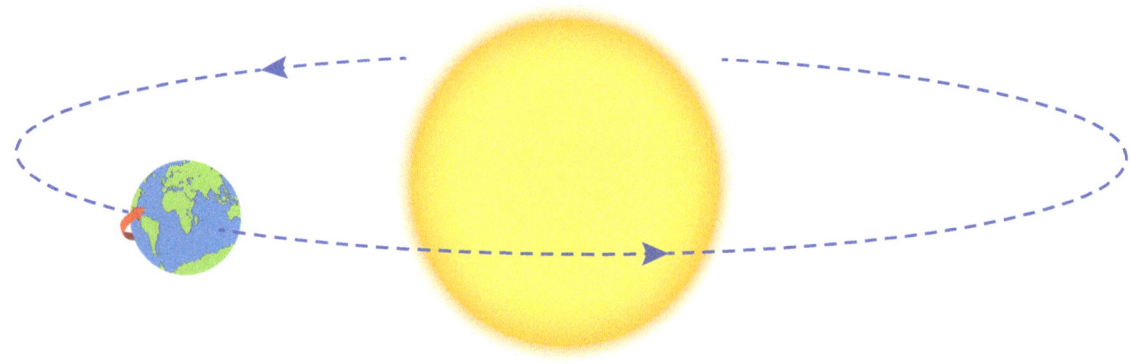

In one year the earth makes one trip around the sun. During that year Earth rotates 365 times. This means that in one year there are 365 days.

Activity
Earth Rotates and Revolves

For this activity, you will need a big ball and a globe.

- ☐ Get a big ball and set it down in an open space. Imagine that the ball is the sun and your body is the earth.

- ☐ Stand by the ball and rotate your body. This is how Earth rotates through days and nights.

- ☐ Now move your body in a complete circle around the ball to make one full trip around the ball. This is how Earth revolves around the sun.

- ☐ Practice rotating and revolving. When you are sure of the difference, show someone else what each word means.

- ☐ Now use a globe to show how Earth rotates through days and nights while it revolves through one full year. You don't have to show all 365 days.

4

The Moon

The **moon** is a large round object that goes around our planet. When we look in the sky at night we can sometimes see it. Once in a while we can see the moon during the day, but it is not as bright as it is at night.

Looking at it, you might think the moon is as large as the sun but it is really much smaller. The moon is even smaller than Earth. The moon *looks* about as large as the sun because it is much closer to Earth than the sun is. The sun is very far away from Earth. Even farther than shown in this picture.

THE MOON

The moon revolves around Earth while Earth is revolving around the sun.

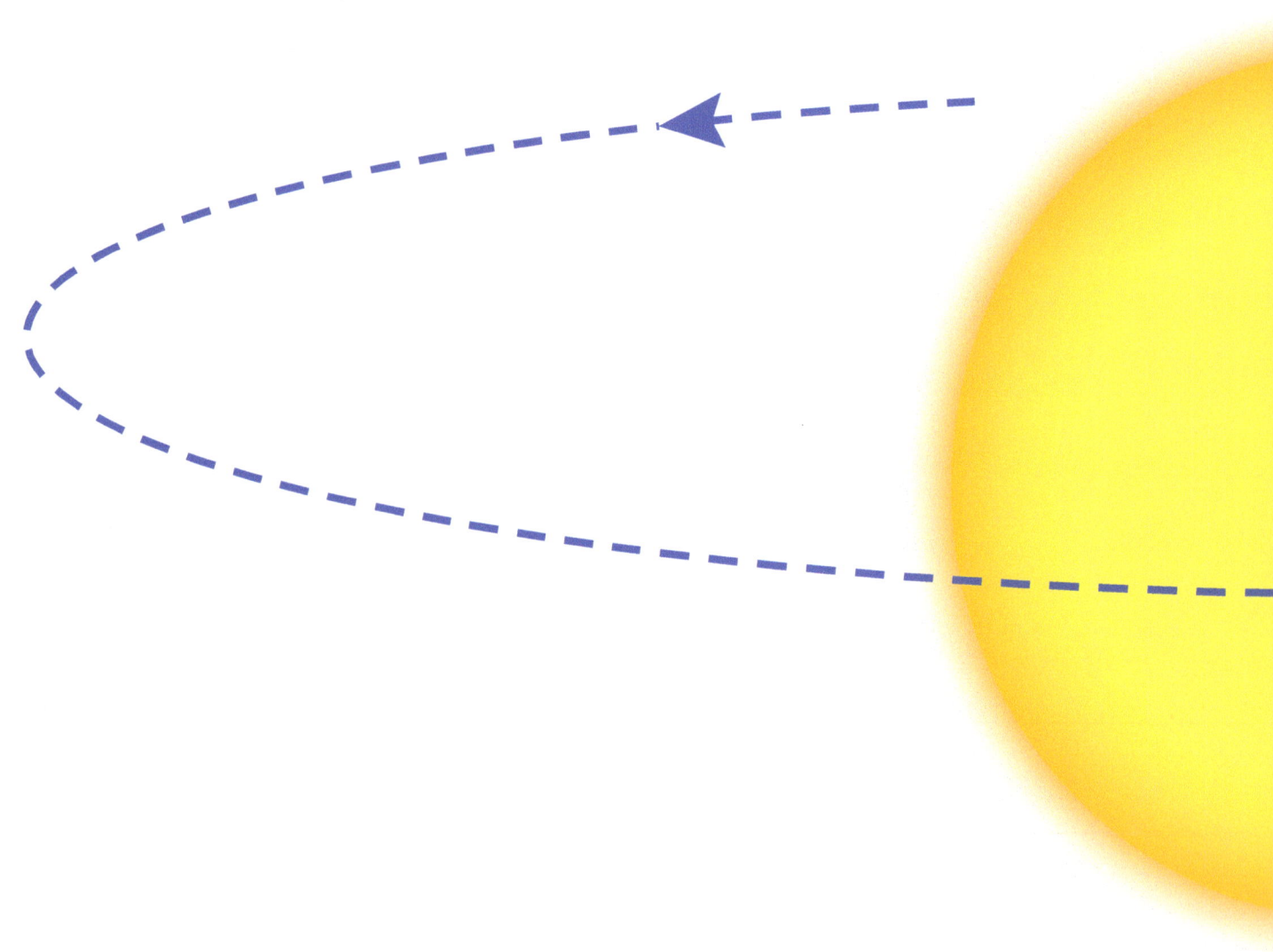

40

THE MOON

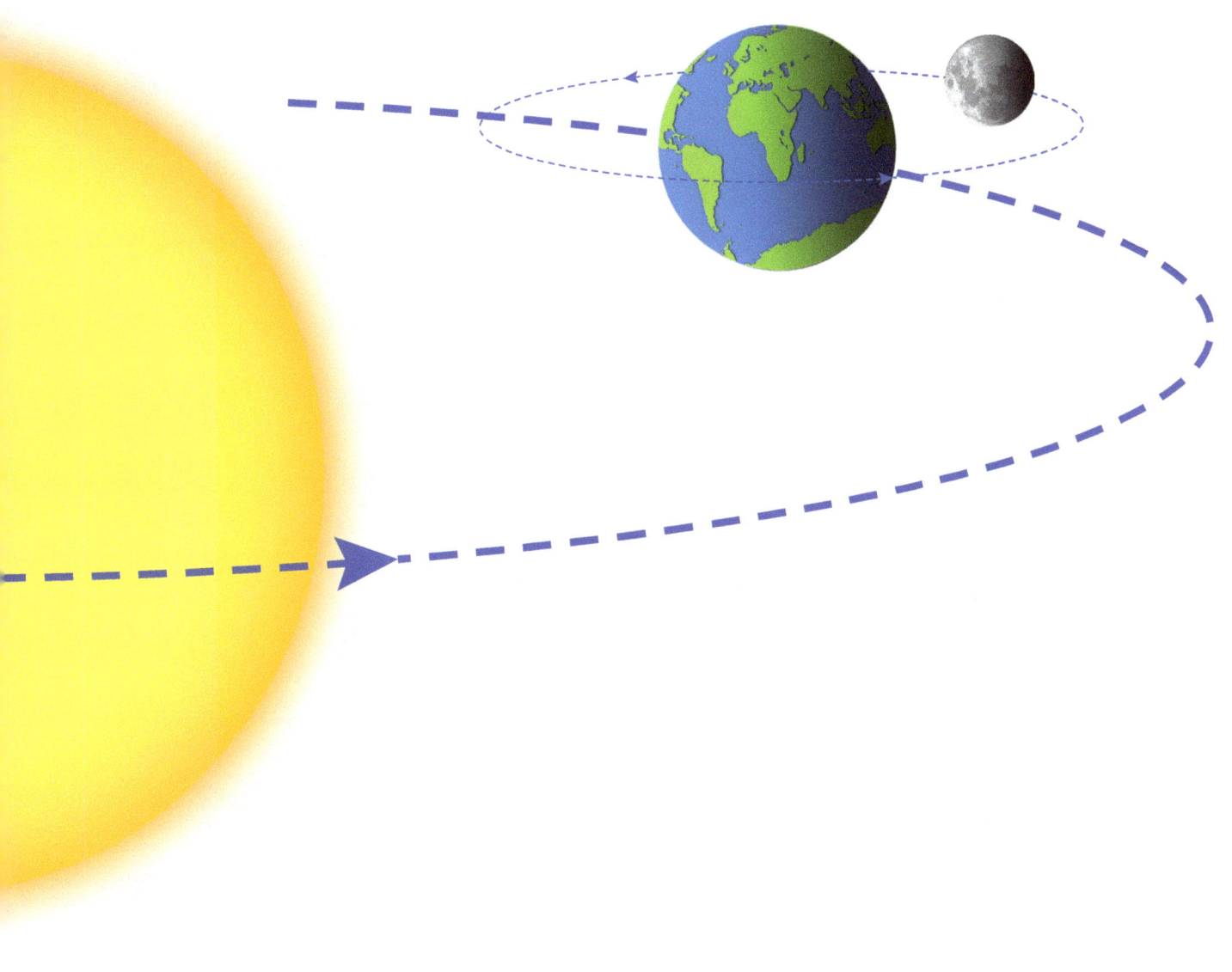

WHAT THE MOON IS LIKE

The moon is made of rock and dirt. It does not have water or air on it. It is all land. There are many mountains on the moon. There are also round dents on the moon called **craters**. When you look at the moon through binoculars, you can see the craters and mountains.

The temperature on the moon is very different from Earth's temperature. Where the sun shines on the moon it is very, very hot. Where the sun doesn't shine, it is very, very cold. Even if there were air to breathe, it would either be too hot or too cold for us to live on the moon.

THE MOON

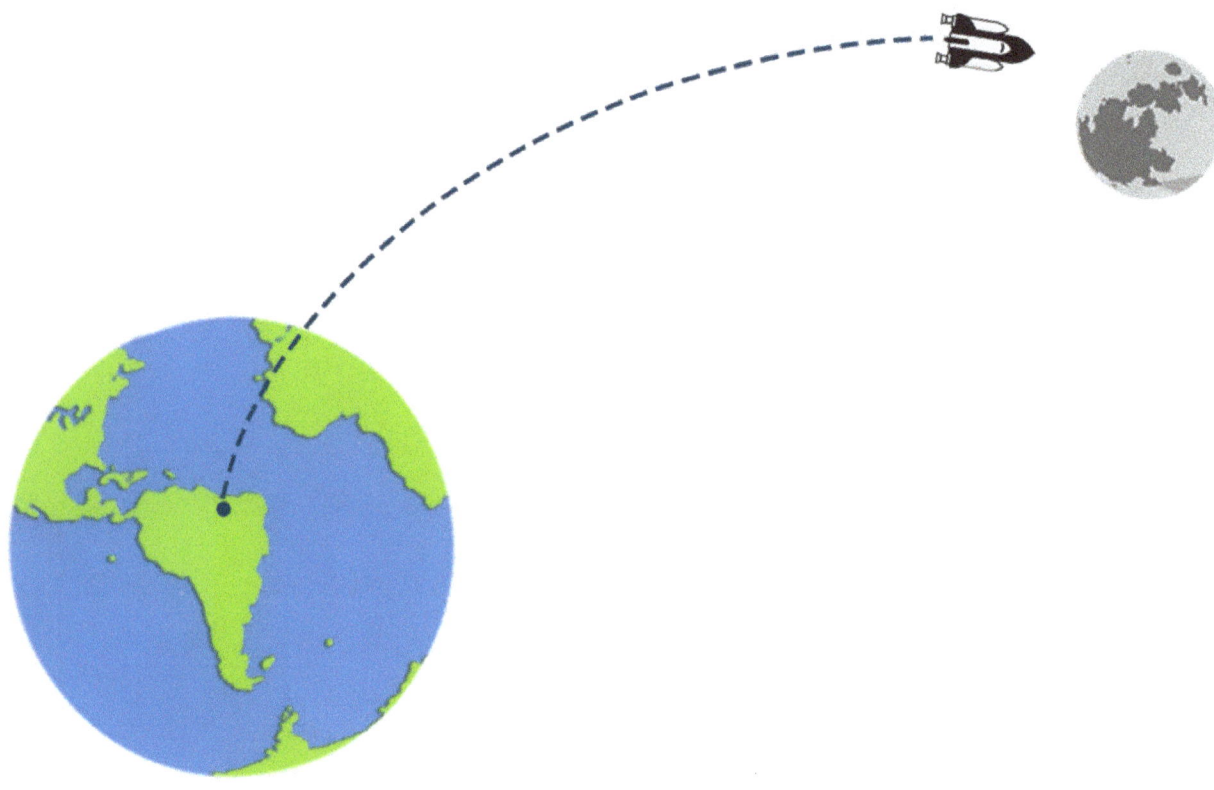

A few people have visited the moon. They made the long trip in a spaceship. It took them three days to get there.

The people who traveled to the moon were called astronauts. When they reached the moon they were able to walk around wearing special suits. The suits protected them from the heat and cold and gave them air to breathe.

The astronauts who went to the moon took pictures and did experiments so that we could learn more about the moon. They even brought back some moon rocks! This picture shows the very first spacecraft on the moon and one of the first two astronauts who walked there.

5
Distances in Space

DISTANCES IN SPACE ARE HUGE

Just to compare, the distance across the United States from the Atlantic Ocean to the Pacific Ocean is almost 3,000 miles. It can take almost seven days to drive across the United States. That includes time to eat and sleep, but it's still a long time.

It's about 25,000 miles all the way around Earth. That's about eight times as far as driving across the United States. If you could drive around the earth it would take you about 60 days. That's two months!

DISTANCES IN SPACE

The moon is about 240,000 miles from Earth. That is nearly as much as 10 trips all the way around Earth. If you could drive there, it would take 550 days to do it. That is about a year and a half, driving every day.

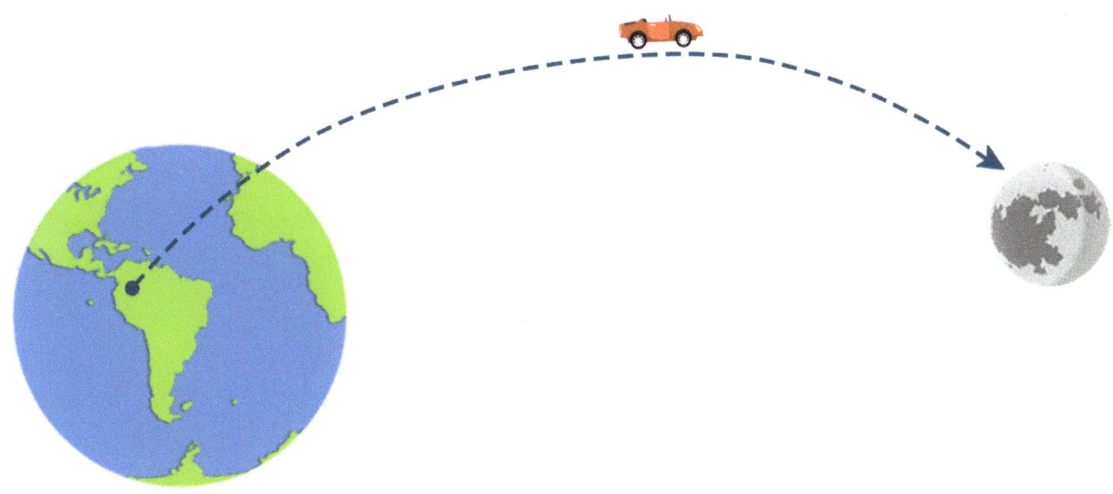

Once you got there, you'd find the moon was smaller than Earth. It's only about 7,000 miles around. You could drive around the moon in only about 15 days. (Remember, it would take 60 days to drive around the earth.)

DISTANCES IN SPACE

The distance to the sun is 93 million miles. That's almost 400 times as far from Earth as the moon is. It would take nearly 600 years to drive to the sun (as long as you don't take any days off). Maybe the car wouldn't last that long. How about the driver?

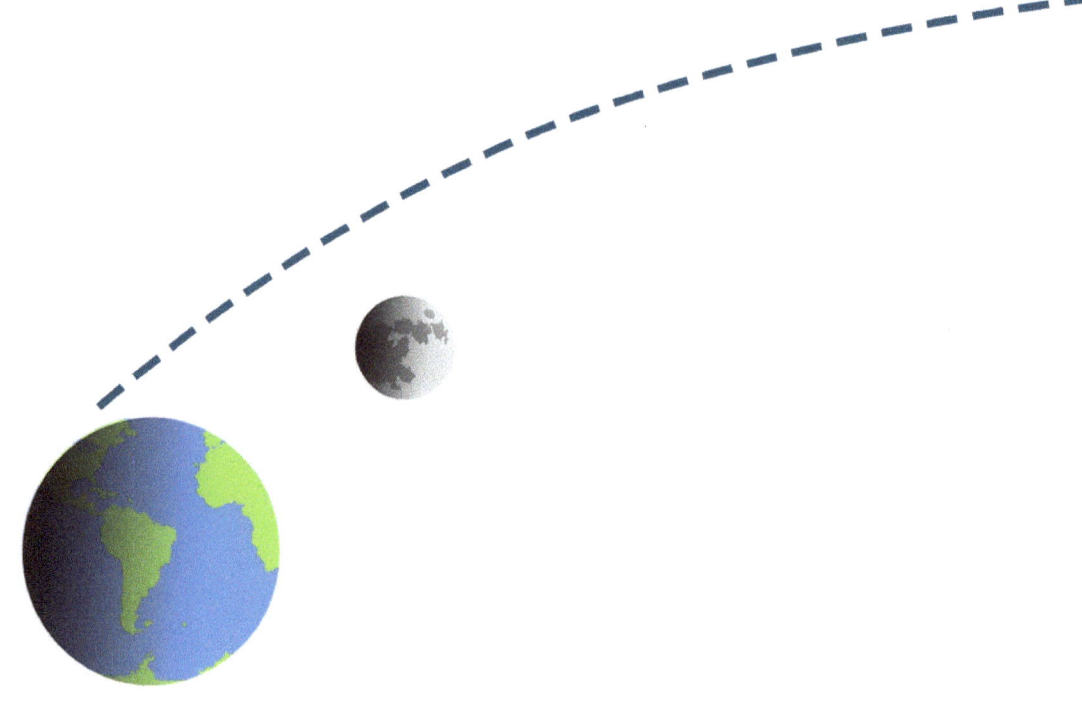

DISTANCES IN SPACE

Once you got to the sun, you'd find it was huge. It's more than 100 times farther around the sun than it is around Earth. If your car was still working, it would take you 17 more years just to drive around the sun!

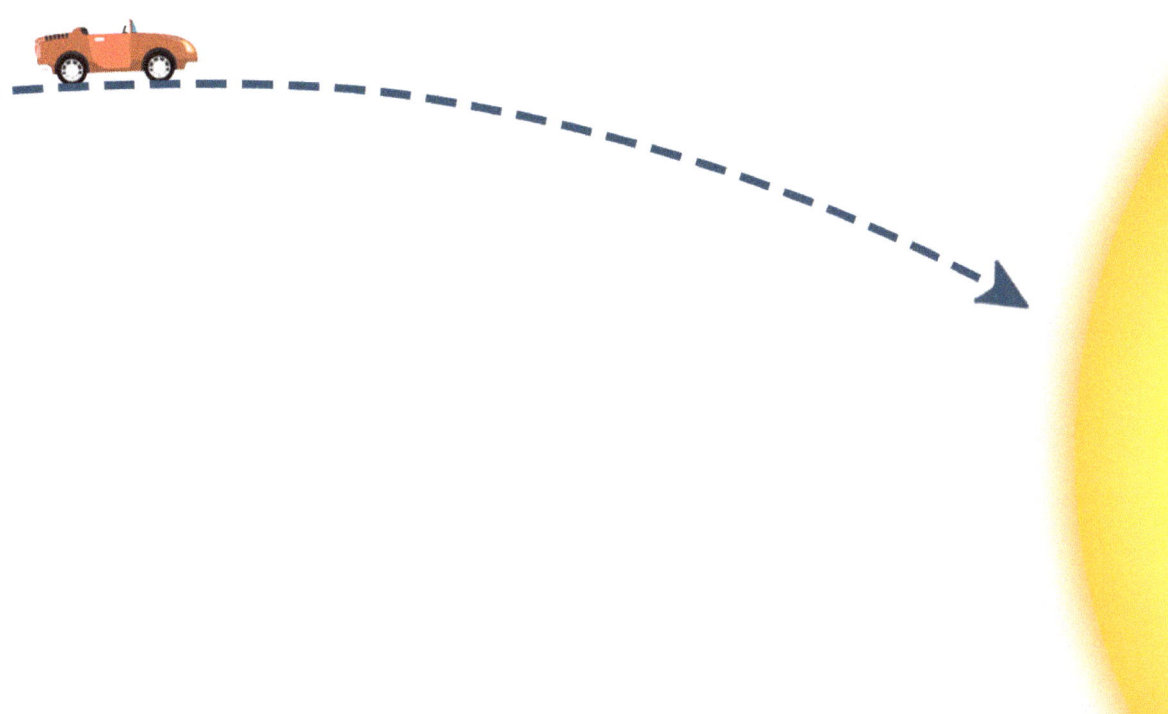

Of course, you can't drive cars through space. When we think about going to the moon or the sun, we don't think about driving. We think about using a spaceship. Remember that it took the astronauts about three days to reach the moon. Spaceships go a lot faster than cars but it would still take about three years to reach the sun.

DISTANCES IN SPACE

Activity
Distances in Space

For this activity, you will need a space at least 140 feet long, two sharpened pencils, measuring tape or yardstick, a marble, a bb or small bead, a basketball and binoculars.

☐ Put the marble down at one end of the space. Lay a pencil next to the marble with the end pointing at the marble.

☐ Put the bb or small bead down about four inches away from the marble. Lay another pencil next to the bead with the end pointing at the bead.

☐ Measure 130 feet from the marble and set the basketball down.

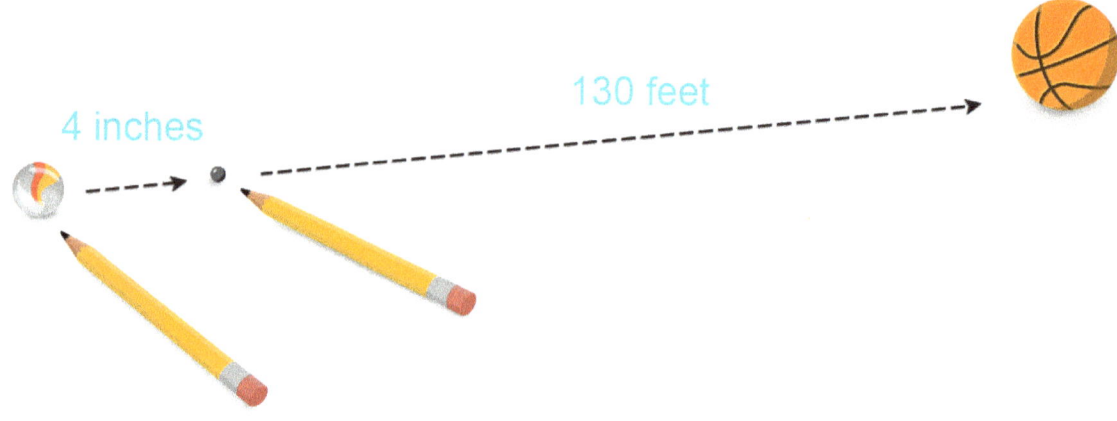

☐ Imagine the basketball is the sun, the marble is Earth and the bb or small bead is the moon.

☐ Standing by the sun, look for Earth and the moon. Can you see them at all?

DISTANCES IN SPACE

- ☐ Now look at Earth and the moon with the binoculars. Can you see them now? You might only be able to see the pencils that point at them, since Earth and the moon are so small.

- ☐ Stand by Earth and the moon. Imagine you are very tiny and standing on Earth. Now look at the sun. Look at the moon.

- ☐ Tell another person what this activity shows about distances in space.

6

How Earth Turns

HOW EARTH TURNS

You could say that Earth is like a top, spinning in space. When a top is spinning, you could imagine that there is a line the top is spinning around, like this.

The line would go right straight down through the center of the top.

Even if the top started to tip over, there would still be a line that it was spinning around. The line would be tipped too, like this.

56

HOW EARTH TURNS

A straight line through the center of an object that the object can turn on is called an **axis**. The line can be real or imaginary.

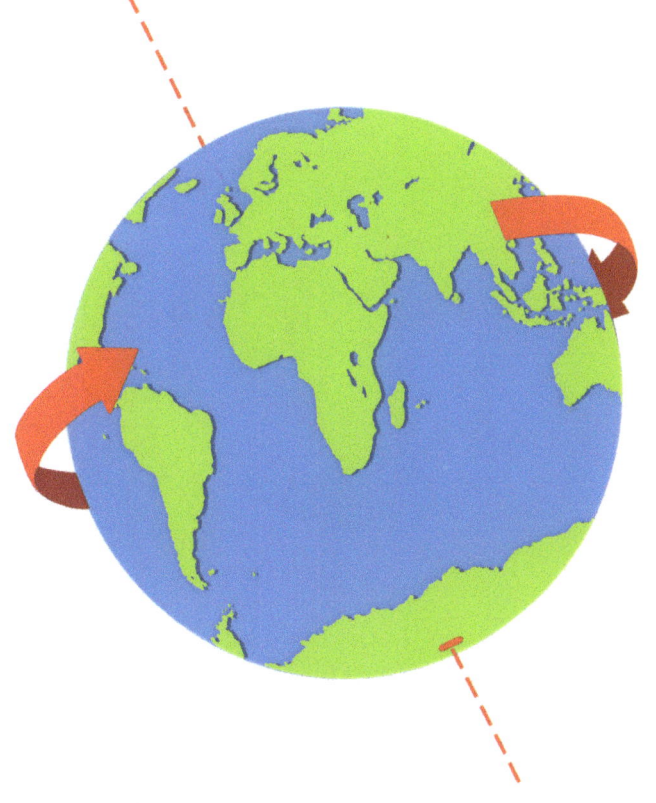

Earth has an axis too, but you can't see it. Earth spins (rotates) on its axis.

Most globes are made so that they can show how Earth rotates. They often have a thin metal bar that goes down through the center of the globe and holds it in place. The globe can spin on the bar. So, you could call the bar the axis if you wanted to but it really just shows where the axis is.

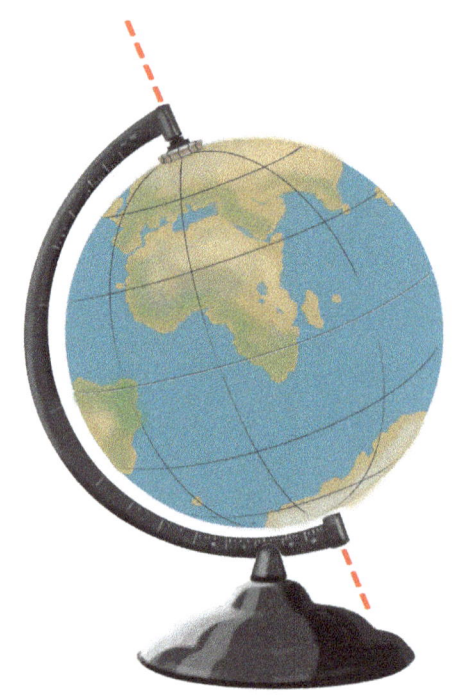

THE NORTH POLE AND THE SOUTH POLE

There are names for the places where the axis comes out of the earth at the top and at the bottom. They are called the **North Pole** and the **South Pole**.

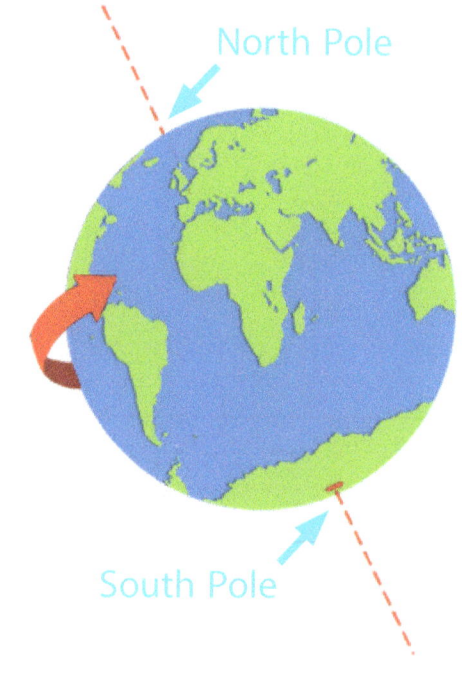

EARTH IS TILTED

Most globes do not show the axis of Earth being straight up and down. They usually show it tilted off to one side. That is because the real earth is tilted compared to the sun. It is not straight up and down.

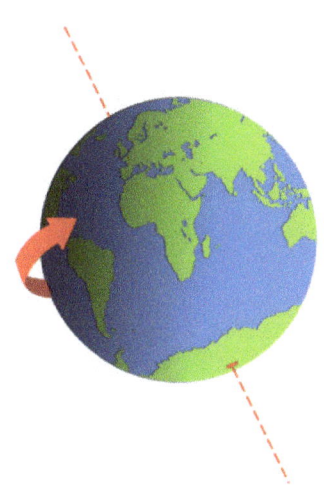

Sometimes drawings of Earth show a line going through the center from top to bottom. The line is there to show where the axis is. Of course, the real earth does not have a line going through it.

HOW EARTH TURNS

Earth rotates on its axis, but it also revolves around the sun. The way Earth is tilted doesn't change when it goes around the sun—it always points in the same direction.

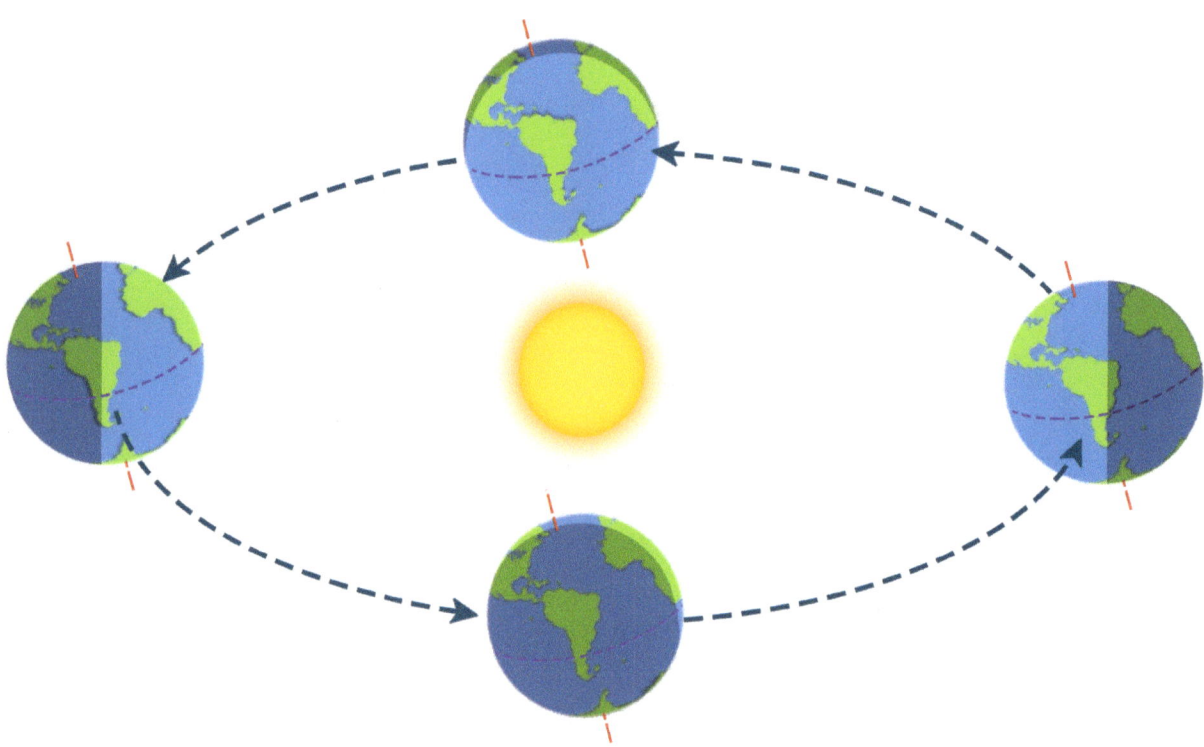

Activity
Earth's Axis Is Tilted

For this activity, you will need a large ball and a globe.

- ☐ Put a large ball in the center of a room. This will be the sun. Put a globe several feet away from it to be Earth.

- ☐ Pick an upper corner of the room. Turn the globe stand until the axis points to that corner.

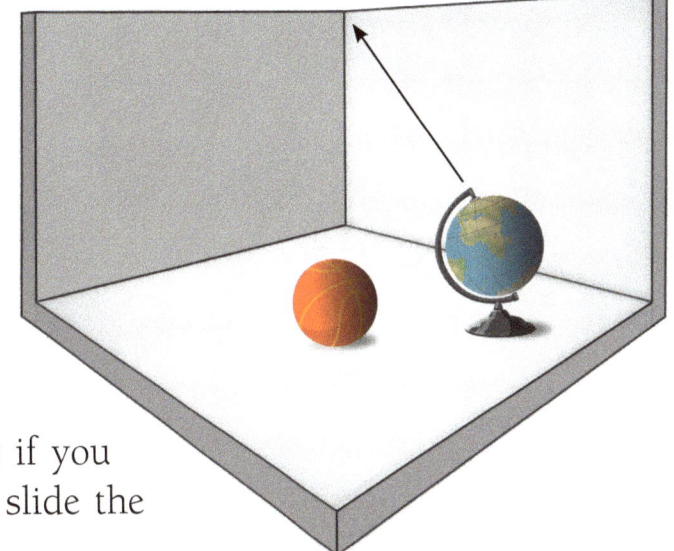

- ☐ Now move Earth around the sun a little bit at a time. As you move it, keep the axis pointed toward the same corner of the room. It can be easier to do this if you keep the stand on the floor and slide the globe without lifting it up.

- ☐ Move Earth this way until it has gone all the way around the sun once. Notice that by always keeping the axis pointed at the same corner of the room, sometimes Earth is tipped *toward* the sun and sometimes it is tipped *away from* the sun.

- ☐ Move Earth all the way around the sun again keeping the axis pointed in the same direction. This time rotate the Earth on its axis as you move it.

- ☐ Explain to someone how this demonstrates Earth moving through days and nights while it goes through a full year.

7
Seasons

THE FOUR SEASONS

It takes one year for Earth to move around the sun. We usually divide a year into four parts called **seasons**. The weather is usually different during each season.

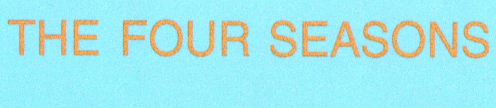

During the season called **summer**, the sun usually shines a lot and it is warm or hot.

When it starts to get cooler, often the leaves turn pretty colors and fall off of the trees. That is the season called **autumn**. Another name for autumn is **fall**.

SEASONS

Winter is the coldest season. In many parts of the world, it snows or rains more in the winter than in other seasons.

After winter, the weather starts to warm up. This is called **spring**. If there is snow, it melts. Flowers start blooming and the trees turn green.

After spring, summer comes again. A whole year has gone by. This means Earth has revolved one full time around the sun. Earth is back to where it started and ready to begin a new year.

HEMISPHERES

The tilt of Earth is what causes the seasons. To talk about that, there are some words it's helpful to know.

The first word is hemisphere. **Hemi-** means "half" and **sphere** is another word for ball. So **hemisphere** means half a ball.

The **equator** is the imaginary line between these two halves or hemispheres.

When you are talking about Earth, a **hemisphere** means half of Earth. The northern half of Earth is called the **Northern Hemisphere**. The southern (SUTH-ern) half is called the **Southern Hemisphere**

SEASONS

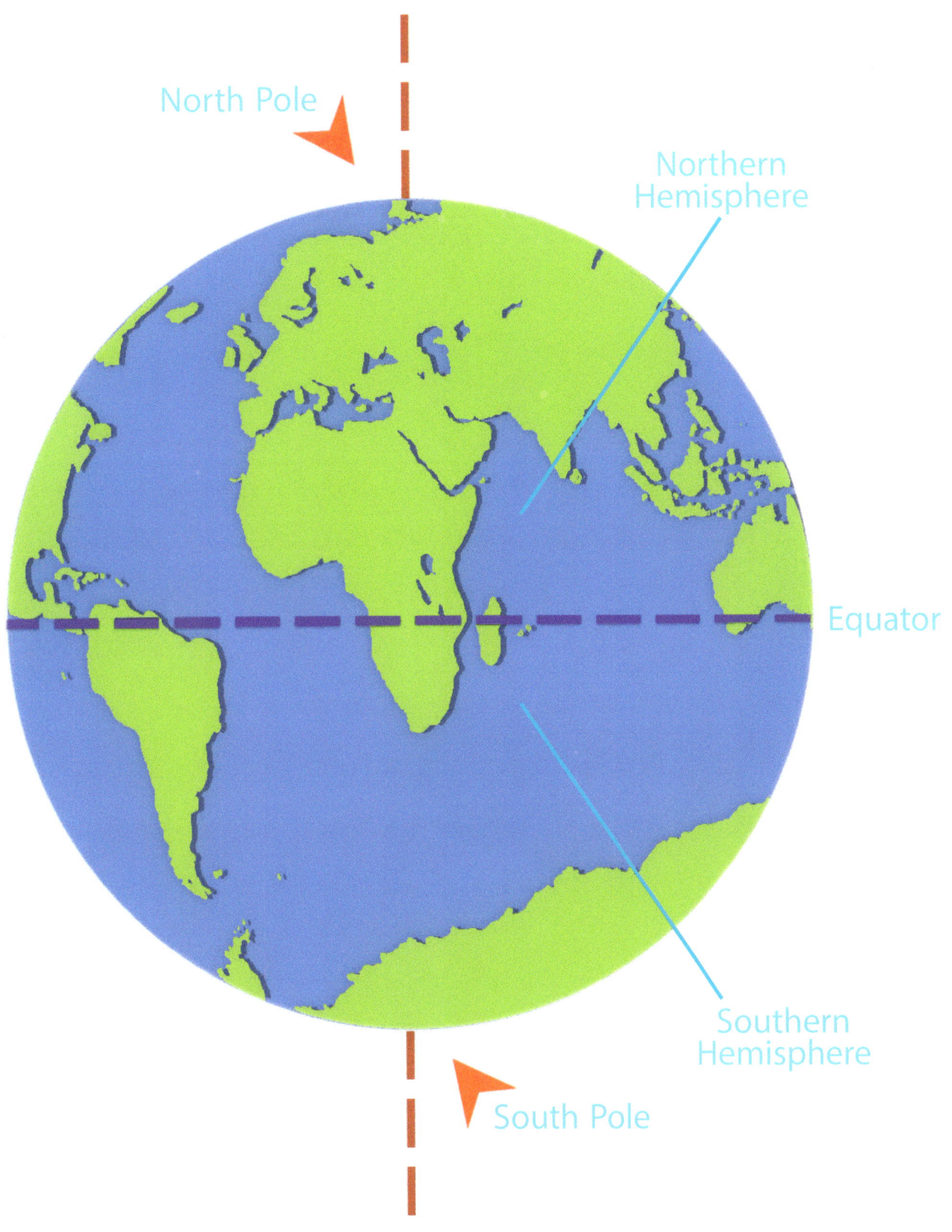

SEASONS

WHAT CAUSES THE SEASONS?

This picture shows Earth going around the sun during one year. Earth is shown in several places on its trip.

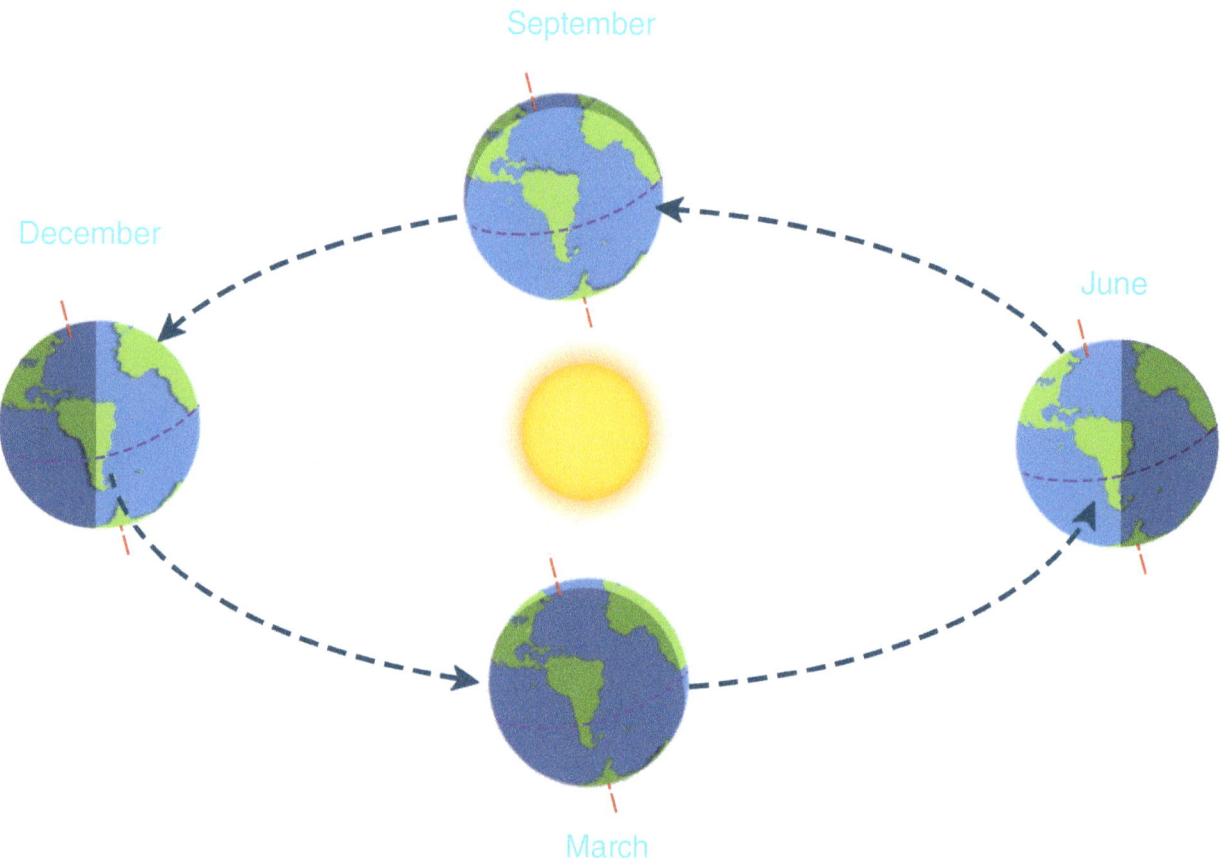

In June, the tilt of the planet causes the sun to shine more strongly on the Northern Hemisphere and less strongly on the Southern Hemisphere. It will be warmer in the Northern Hemisphere and colder in the Southern Hemisphere.

This means that when Earth is in that position, the people in the Northern Hemisphere are having summer and the people in the Southern Hemisphere are having winter.

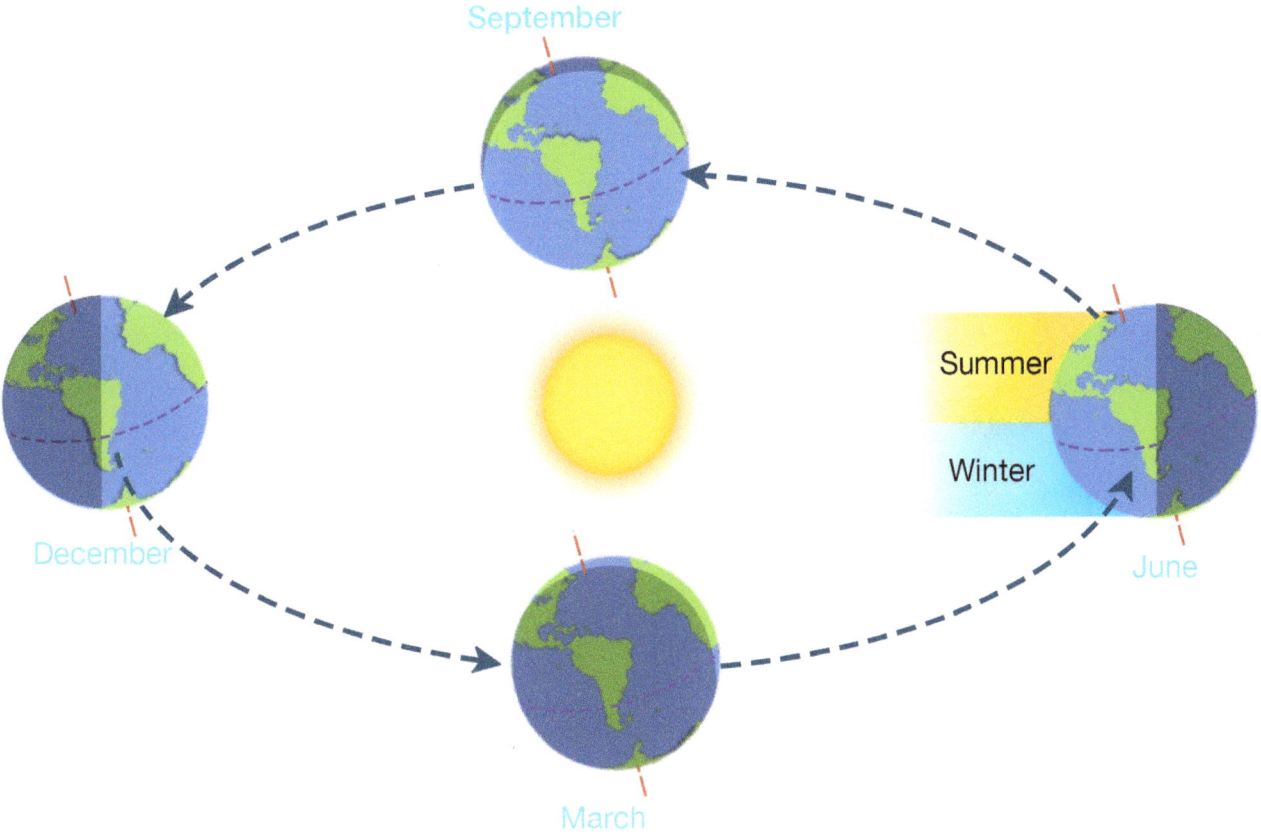

SEASONS

Now look at the picture of Earth in December. The axis is tilted away from the sun in the north. This means the sun is shining *less* strongly north of the equator and is shining more strongly south of the equator. Now the Southern Hemisphere is having summer and the Northern Hemisphere is having winter.

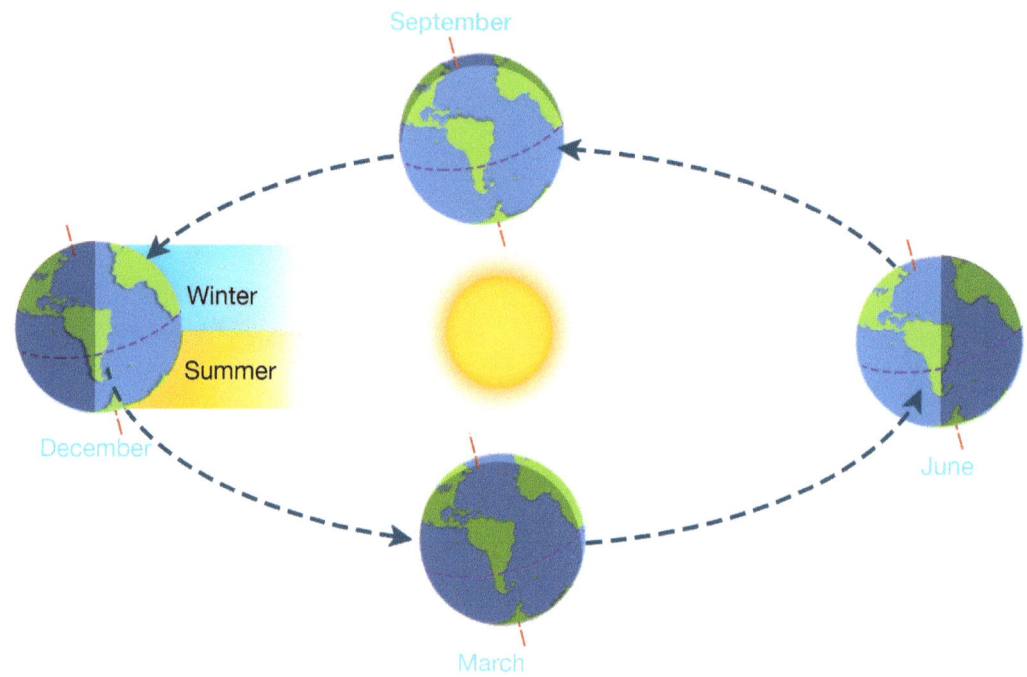

What happens in between? If you look at the picture of Earth in September, you can see that the sun shines about the same in the north as in the south. It is spring in the south and fall in the north.

Now look at Earth in March, and see if you can figure out what season it is in the Northern Hemisphere and in the Southern Hemisphere.

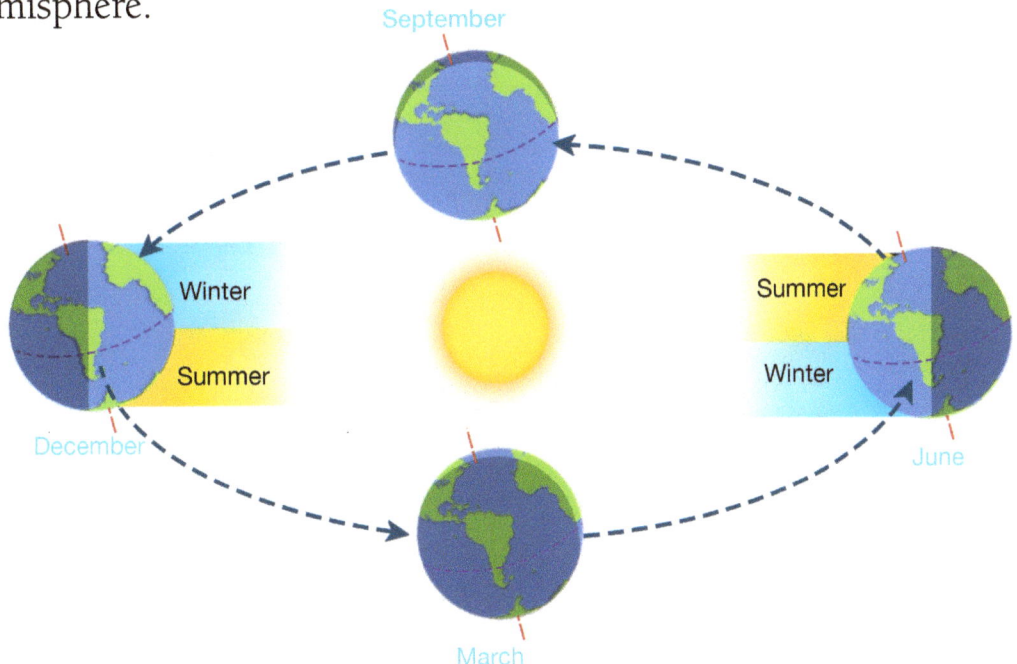

If you said "spring" in the north and "fall" in the south, you are right!

Each time Earth makes one trip around the sun a year has passed. And because the axis of Earth is tilted and always points the same way, the seasons repeat over and over again.

SEASONS

Activity
What Causes the Seasons?

For this activity, you will need a globe and a small lamp without a shade.

☐ Put a small lamp without a shade in the center of a room to be the sun. Place a globe several feet away. The bulb of the lamp should be at the same height as the center of the globe.

☐ Pick an upper corner of the room. Turn the globe stand until the axis points to that corner.

☐ Turn on the lamp and turn off the other lights in the room.

☐ Show Earth moving around the sun with its axis always tilted toward the corner you chose. As you do this, stop every once in a while and notice which hemisphere is getting the strongest sunlight from the lamp.

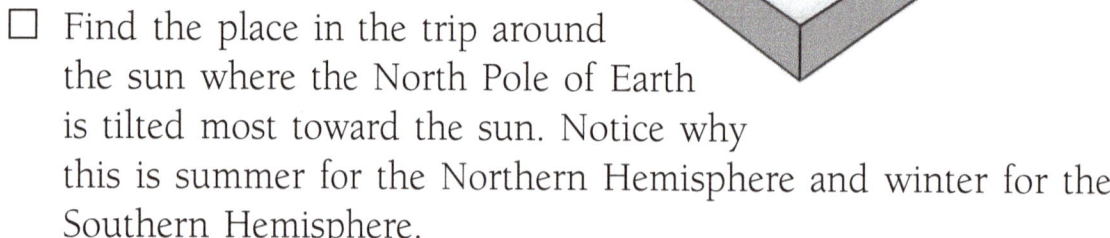

☐ Find the place in the trip around the sun where the North Pole of Earth is tilted most toward the sun. Notice why this is summer for the Northern Hemisphere and winter for the Southern Hemisphere.

SEASONS

☐ Find the place in the trip around the sun where the North Pole is tilted away from the sun. Notice why this is winter for the Northern Hemisphere and summer for the Southern Hemisphere.

☐ Keep moving the earth around the sun. Decide which position is spring for the Northern Hemisphere. Notice what is happening in the Southern Hemisphere then.

☐ Decide which position is fall for the Northern Hemisphere. Notice what is happening in the Southern Hemisphere then.

☐ Move the globe around the sun again so that it is in the December position.

☐ Rotate the globe through a day and a night. Notice that this shows a winter day and winter night in the Northern Hemisphere, and a summer day and summer night in the Southern Hemisphere.

☐ On the globe, find a place in the Northern Hemisphere. Think of an activity people there might be doing in December. Now find a place in the Southern Hemisphere. Think of an activity people there might be doing in December. Tell your teacher what you thought of.

☐ Decide what season you are having now and then work out in your demonstration where the earth is in order for it to be that season.

The Way the Moon Looks

THE WAY THE MOON LOOKS

If you watch the moon night after night, it seems to change shape. Actually, the moon is always round. What changes is how much of the moon we can see.

A **full moon** is the shape of the moon when it looks like this.

A **half moon** looks like this.

Or this.

THE WAY THE MOON LOOKS

A **crescent moon** looks like this.

Or this.

A **new moon** is what we call the moon when it is all dark. It looks like no moon at all! Sometimes we can see a faint line around the edge.

The different ways that the moon can look are called **phases**.

PHASES OF THE MOON

After a full moon, the moon looks as if it is getting smaller and smaller every night until it becomes a new moon.

This takes about 15 days.

After a new moon, the moon looks as if it is getting bigger and bigger every night until it becomes a full moon again

This also takes about 15 days.

Then the phases start all over again. It takes about one month for the moon to go through all its phases.

Why the Moon Seems to Change

WHY THE MOON SEEMS TO CHANGE

The moon revolves around Earth in one month. And, during the month it seems to change. But why?

We see the moon because the sun shines on it. The moon does not make any light of its own. The light we see from the moon is reflected from the sun. That means light from the sun hits the moon and bounces back to Earth. That is the moonlight we see.

WHY THE MOON SEEMS TO CHANGE

When it is nighttime and we cannot see the sun, sunlight is still shining on the moon. That is why we can often see the moon at night.

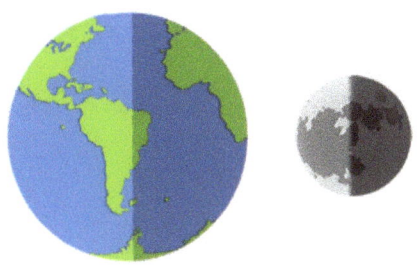

The part of the moon facing the sun is always lit up by the sun. As the moon moves around Earth, we see different parts of the lighted side. How much of the moon we see depends on where it is in its four-week trip around the Earth.

WHY THE MOON SEEMS TO CHANGE

Let's look again at the phases of the moon.

When we see the full circle of the moon, it is called a **full moon**.

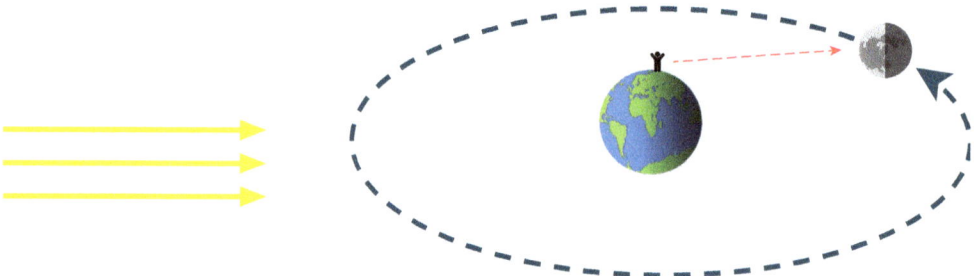

During a full moon, a person on the dark side of Earth where it is night sees the whole face of the moon lit up.

After about a week, the moon moves enough that you can see only half of the lighted side of the moon from Earth.

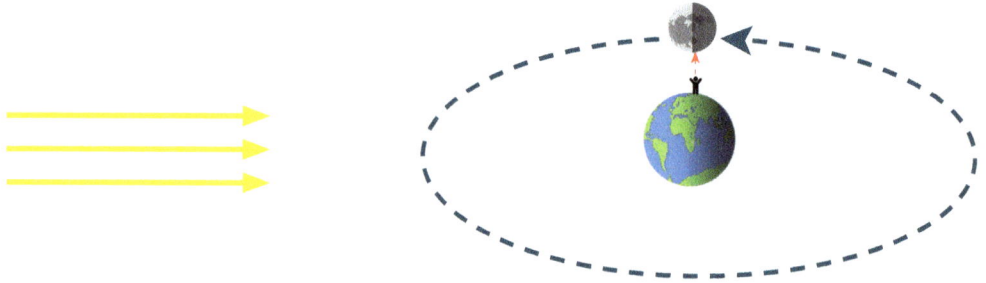

It looks like half of the moon is light and half of it is dark. We call this a "**half moon**."

86

WHY THE MOON SEEMS TO CHANGE

The moon continues to revolve around Earth. About five days later most of the moon facing the person is dark and you can only see a small part of the lighted side. This shape of the moon is called a **crescent moon** because it is in the shape of a crescent.

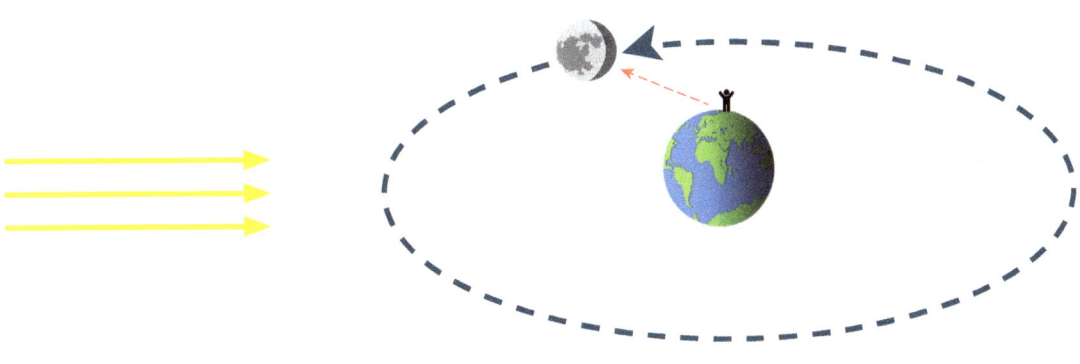

The moon continues to revolve around Earth. Two or three days later you can't see the lighted side at all. The moon is completely dark because the lighted side is facing the sun and the dark side is facing Earth. When the moon is like this, we say it is a **new moon**.

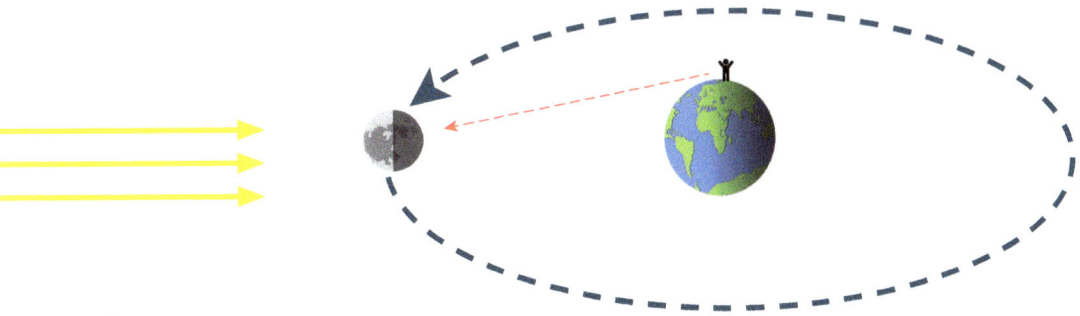

About 15 days have passed and the moon has now traveled half way around Earth from where we started.

WHY THE MOON SEEMS TO CHANGE

Two or three days later we can see a crescent moon again, but now it is on the *other* side.

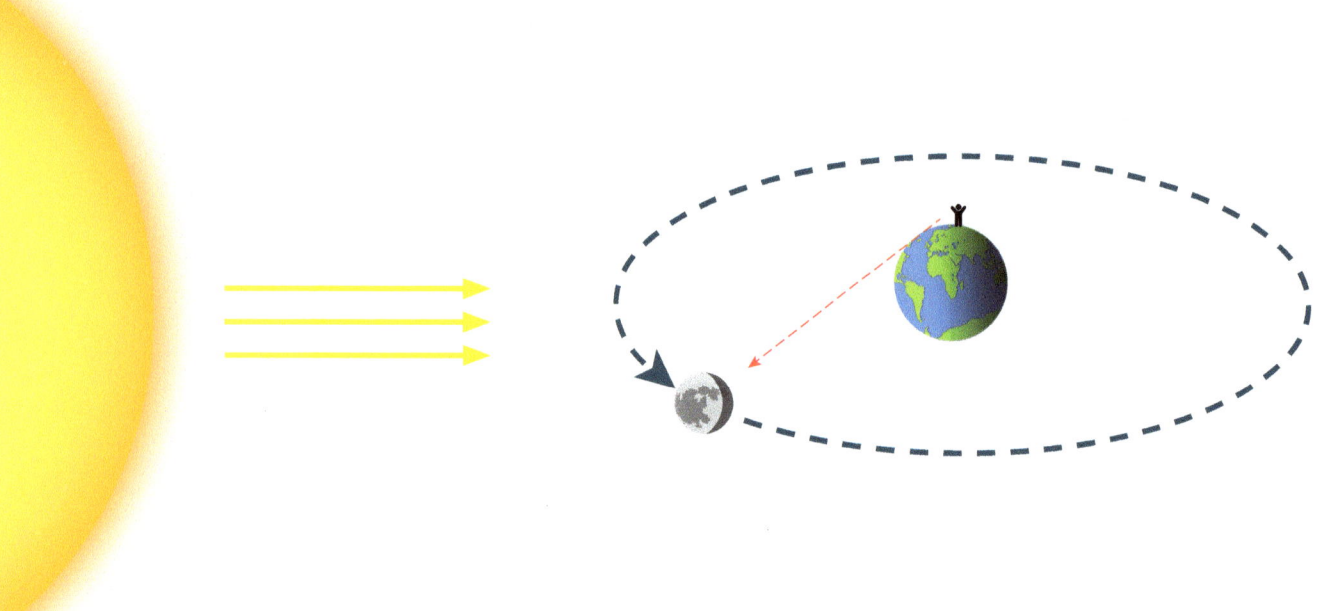

About five days later you can see a half moon again, but now it is facing left just as the second crescent moon did.

Another week passes and the moon moves all the way around to where we started. Now we can see the full moon again. It has been about 30 days since the last full moon.

Activity
Why the Moon Seems to Change

For this activity, you will need a large ball and a small lamp without a shade.

☐ Set a small lamp without a shade on a shelf a bit higher than your head.

☐ Turn on the lamp and hold a large ball high with your back to the light. Be sure to hold the ball with your arm straight out and up just a bit so that your body doesn't block any of the light. Imagine the lamp is the sun and the ball is the moon.

☐ Notice how the light shines on part of the ball, but the rest of the ball is in shadow. Now have your teacher hold the ball the same way. You walk around the ball and notice how much of the ball is in shadow and how much is in the light.

WHY THE MOON SEEMS TO CHANGE

☐ Now you hold the ball again. Pretend you are looking at the moon from Earth.

☐ Start with a "full moon," where you can see the whole lighted side.

☐ Keep your arm straight and watch the ball while you slowly rotate your body while keeping the ball in the light. Notice how the lighted part of the moon changes.

☐ Stop when you see a "half moon."

☐ Then start rotating again until you see a "crescent moon."

☐ Keep going until you see all of the phases of the moon.

10 Orbits and Planets

ORBITS AND PLANETS

ORBITS

The path a planet follows around its sun is called an **orbit**. Earth takes about 365 days (a year) to go through its whole orbit around the sun.

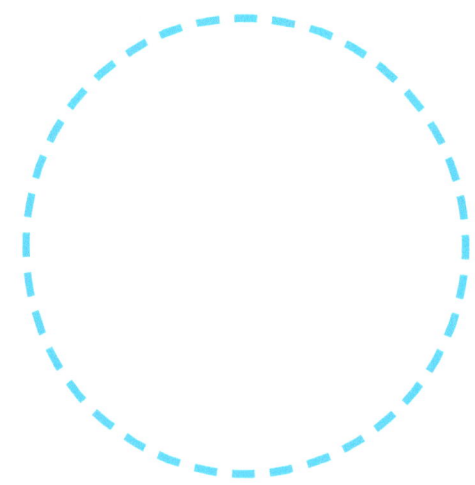

Some orbits are like circles. Others are more like ovals. Another word for oval is **ellipse**.

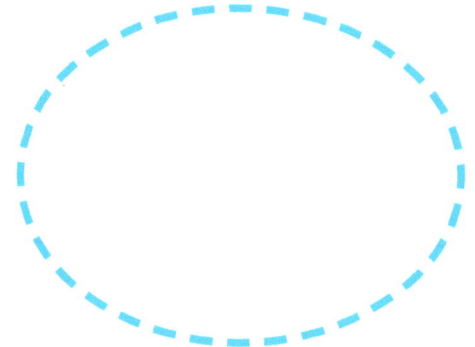

ORBITS AND PLANETS

The orbit of Earth around the sun is not a completely round circle. It is close to a circle but is very slightly flattened, so it is an ellipse.

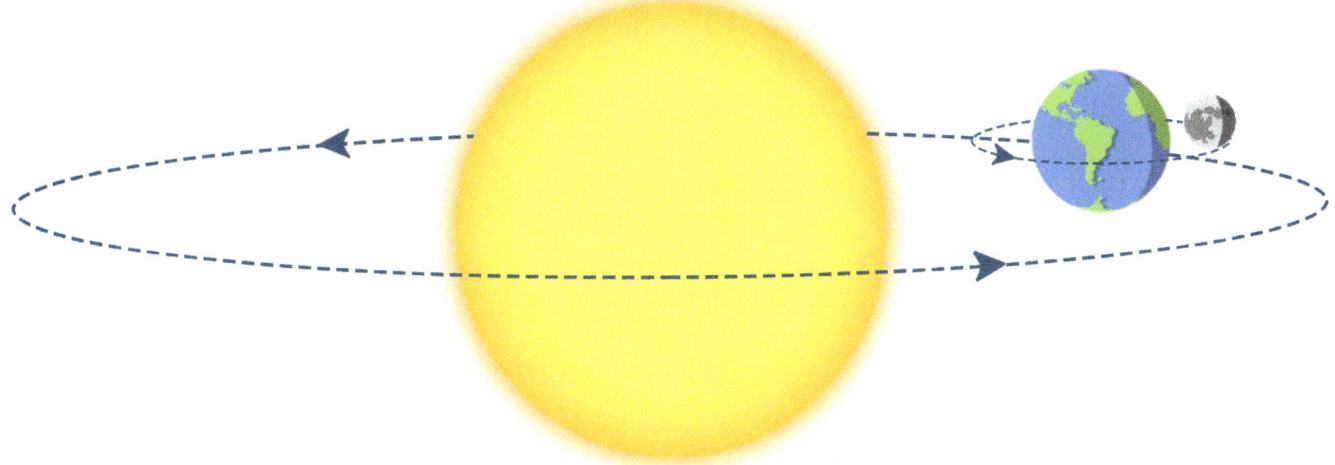

The orbit of the moon around Earth is also an ellipse. It is very close to a circle but not quite. It takes the moon about 30 days to go through its whole orbit around Earth.

There are many other planets in our solar system, each with its own orbit around the sun.

ORBITS AND PLANETS

PLANETS

Earth is one of the eight planets that go around the sun.

Here is a list of the planets from closest to farthest from the sun.

Mercury is first, followed by Venus, Earth, Mars, Jupiter, Saturn, Uranus, and Neptune. Pluto used to be called a planet, but it is so small that today it is called a "dwarf planet."

The planets each move around the sun in an orbit. Some of the orbits are quite round and some are not as round.

Of course you can't really see the orbits. They are just the paths the planets follow around the sun. But if you could draw lines when the planets went around their orbits, the lines would look about like this:

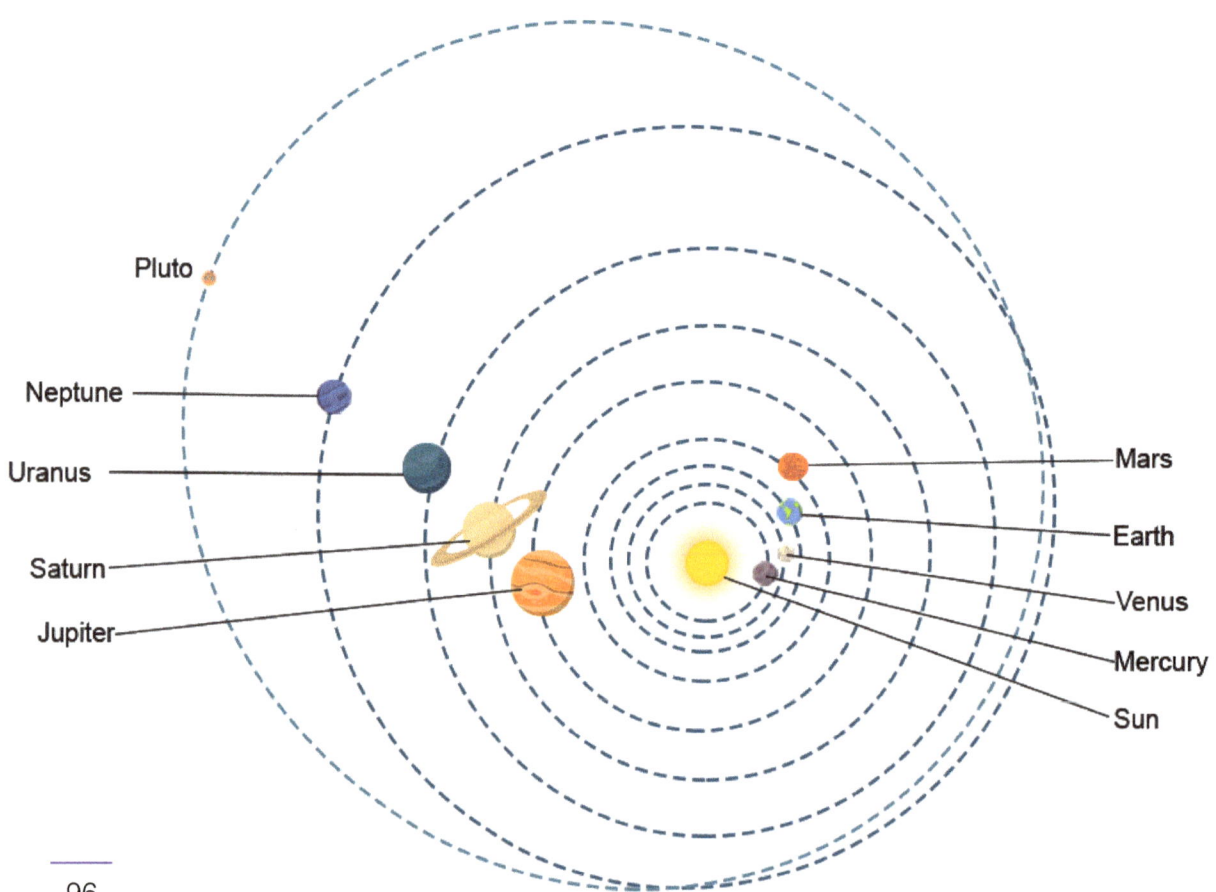

ORBITS AND PLANETS

How big are the orbits? They are huge! The distance from the sun to Earth is 93 million miles and you can see that the distance to Pluto is a *lot* bigger. The orbit of Pluto is about 7 *billion* miles across. Even though the sun and the planets are big, they are small compared to the space between them.

What holds the planets in their orbits and keeps them from just flying off into space? It is the sun. The sun and the planets are so big and heavy that they pull other things toward them. This pull is called gravity. It's the same thing that holds us on Earth.

The sun is larger than all the planets together so it has very strong gravity. It holds the planets around it with the pull of its gravity.

11 The Solar System

THE SOLAR SYSTEM

A **system** is a group of things that together make up a whole thing that is bigger. Our sun and all the planets that go around it in orbits are called the **Solar System.**

THE SUN

A **star** is a huge, burning object in space. Our sun is a star. It is so large that almost a million Earths could fit inside it. Some people call the sun our daytime star because it is the only star we can see in the daytime.

The sun gives light and heat to Earth. Without it there would be no life on Earth.

Sun

THE SOLAR SYSTEM

THE PLANETS

There are two planets closer to the sun than Earth, and five that are farther from the sun.

The planets Mercury and Venus are closer to the sun than Earth and are super-hot because they are so near the sun. They are too hot for people to live there.

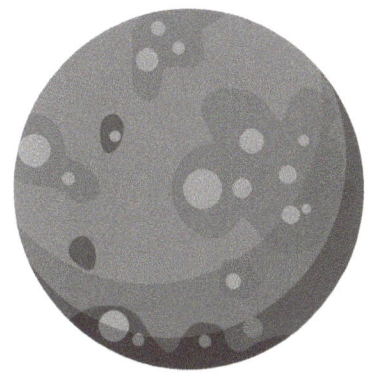

Mercury

Mercury is like a super-hot, dry desert.

Venus

Venus is always covered with super-hot poisonous clouds.

THE SOLAR SYSTEM

After Earth is Mars. Mars is sometimes called the Red Planet. It is smaller than Earth—it is only a little more than half the size of Earth. Mars doesn't have oceans and it doesn't have much air, but it has a large area of ice similar to Earth's North Pole.

Mars

Because it is farther from the sun than Earth, it is colder. But it is still warm enough that there could be some kinds of animals or plants or tiny creatures living near the surface, if there was enough air and water.

Scientists are working to find out what is on Mars, but right now we still don't know for sure.

THE SOLAR SYSTEM

The planets beyond Mars are Jupiter, Saturn, Uranus and Neptune. The dwarf planet, Pluto, is beyond Neptune. These planets are a long, long way from the sun and usually are very, very cold.

Two that are interesting are Jupiter and Saturn.

Jupiter

Jupiter is the largest of our planets. It is about 11 times larger than Earth and is so big that more than a thousand Earths could fit in it. The outer parts of it are very cold, but the center of Jupiter is very hot like our sun.

Saturn is a large planet too, but not as big as Jupiter. It is very cold and has beautiful rings around it, which might be made up of little pieces of ice and dust.

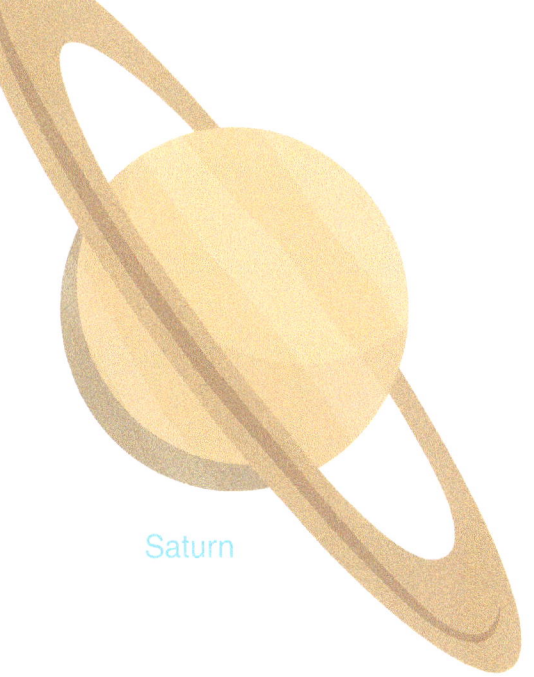

Saturn

THE SOLAR SYSTEM

MOONS

A **moon** is a large round object that orbits a planet. Most of the planets in our solar system have moons. Earth has only one moon, but Jupiter has at least 14 moons!

THE SOLAR SYSTEM

SOME PLANETS CAN LOOK LIKE STARS

The sun shines on all the planets just like it shines on Earth and on our moon. The sun shines on the half of the planet that is facing the sun, but the other half of the planet is dark. If we can see the lighted half of a planet when the sun is shining on it, it will look like a star in the sky to us on Earth.

In this picture Mars would look like a star in our night sky.

We can often see Venus shining in the morning around sunrise and in the evening around sunset. Sometimes we can see other planets too.

12
Asteroids and Falling Stars

ASTEROIDS AND FALLING STARS

ASTEROIDS

The word **asteroid** means "like a star." Asteroids are big rocks. They revolve around the sun, just as the planets do.

Between Mars and Jupiter, there are lots of asteroids going in their own orbits around the sun. This is called the **asteroid belt** because it is a bit like a belt around the sun. There are millions of asteroids in it.

Sometimes asteroids get loose from the asteroid belt. Some asteroids have come close enough to Earth to crash into the moon. This made round dents and holes on the moon. These holes are called **craters**.

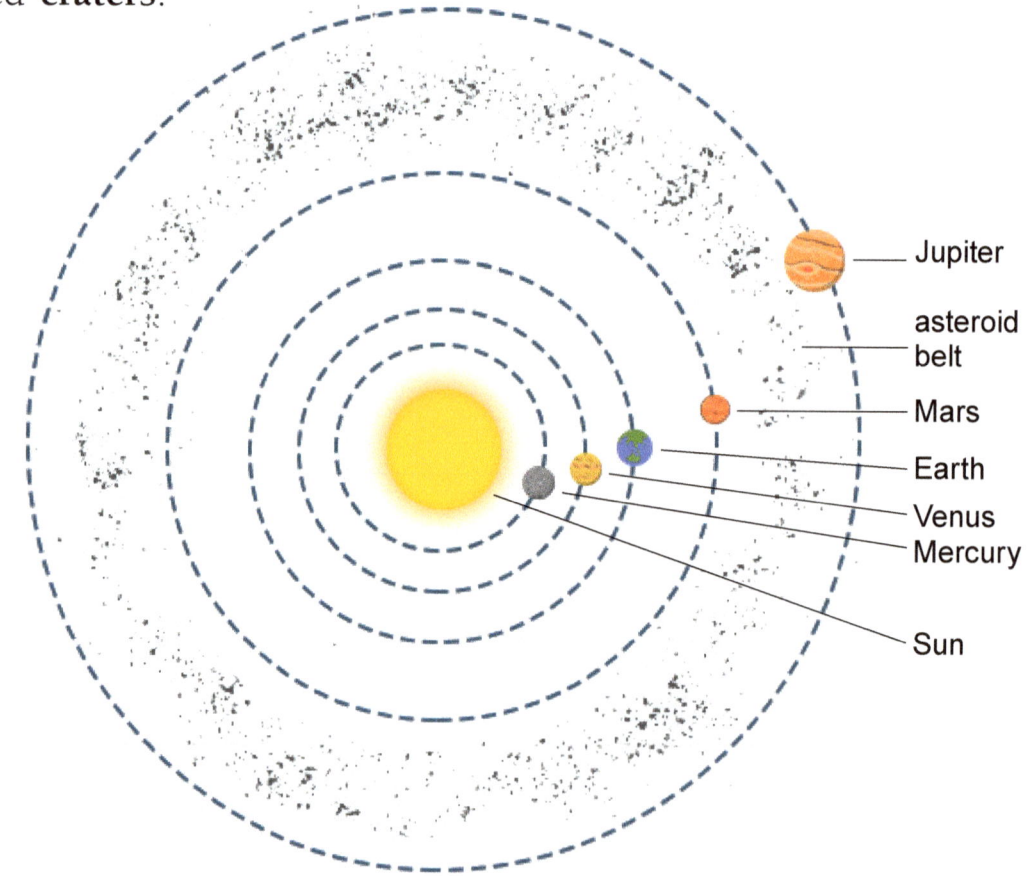

FALLING STARS

When you are looking at the sky at night you can occasionally see something that looks like a bright light streaking toward the ground. These streaks of light are often called **falling stars** or **shooting stars**.

Falling stars (or shooting stars) are not really stars at all. They are tiny asteroids that are burning as they rush through Earth's air.

Sometimes asteroids get into orbits that send them right toward Earth. They fall very, very fast. As they pass through Earth's atmosphere they get very hot. This is because the atmosphere is rubbing against them as they fall. When you rub things together very fast, they get hot. The asteroids get so hot they catch on fire and they burn up, even though they are rocks.

METEORS

Another name for a falling star is **meteor**.

Most meteors burn up before they touch Earth. Some larger meteors are too big to burn up, so they make it all the way through the atmosphere and hit the ground. After they hit the ground they are called **meteorites**

Sometimes large numbers of meteors hit Earth's atmosphere about the same time and you can see many falling stars, one after another, lasting for hours. This is called a meteor shower. It usually happens late at night.

About 50,000 years ago a very large meteor hit Earth in Arizona. It made a hole about a mile across! This hole is called Meteor Crater.

If you visit Arizona, you may get a chance to go to the Meteor Crater and see how huge it really is.

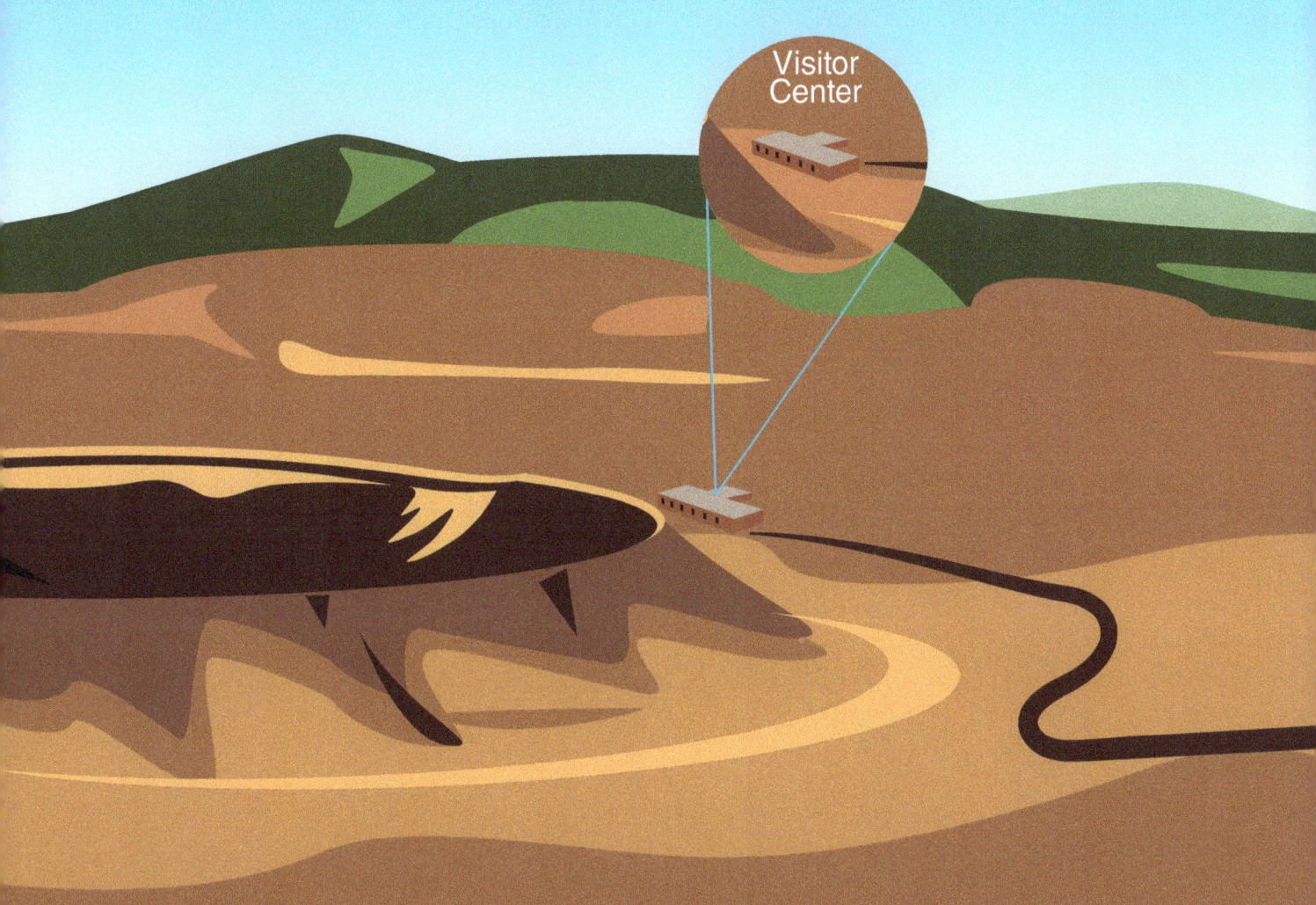

13
Comets

COMETS

A **comet** is a ball of rock, dust and ice traveling through space. Comets are not very big, maybe a mile or so across. That is *much* smaller than the moon.

COMETS

A comet moves in an orbit around the sun. The orbit is usually a very long ellipse that brings the comet close to the sun, then carries it out to the very edge of the solar system before it starts back toward the sun again.

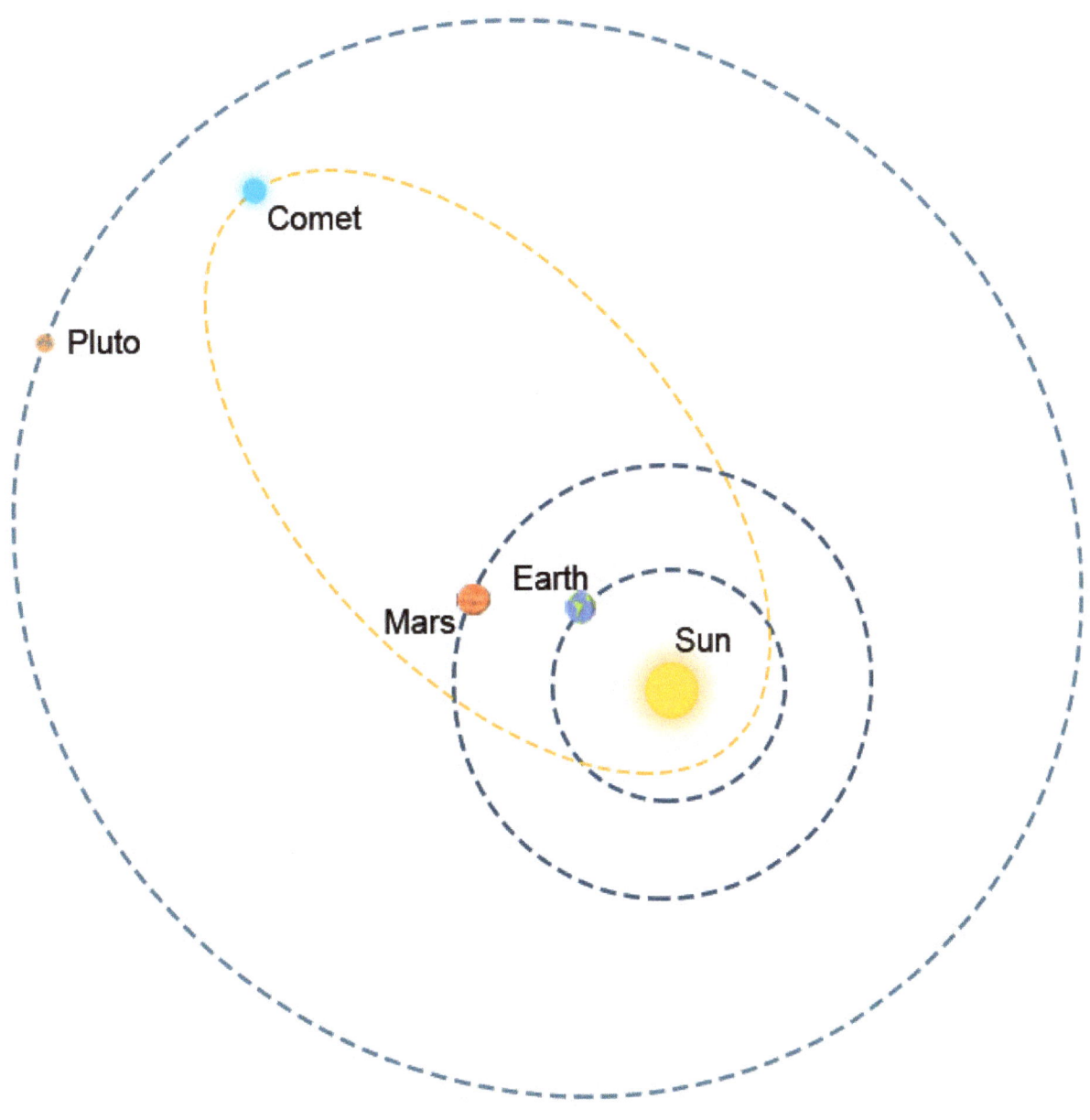

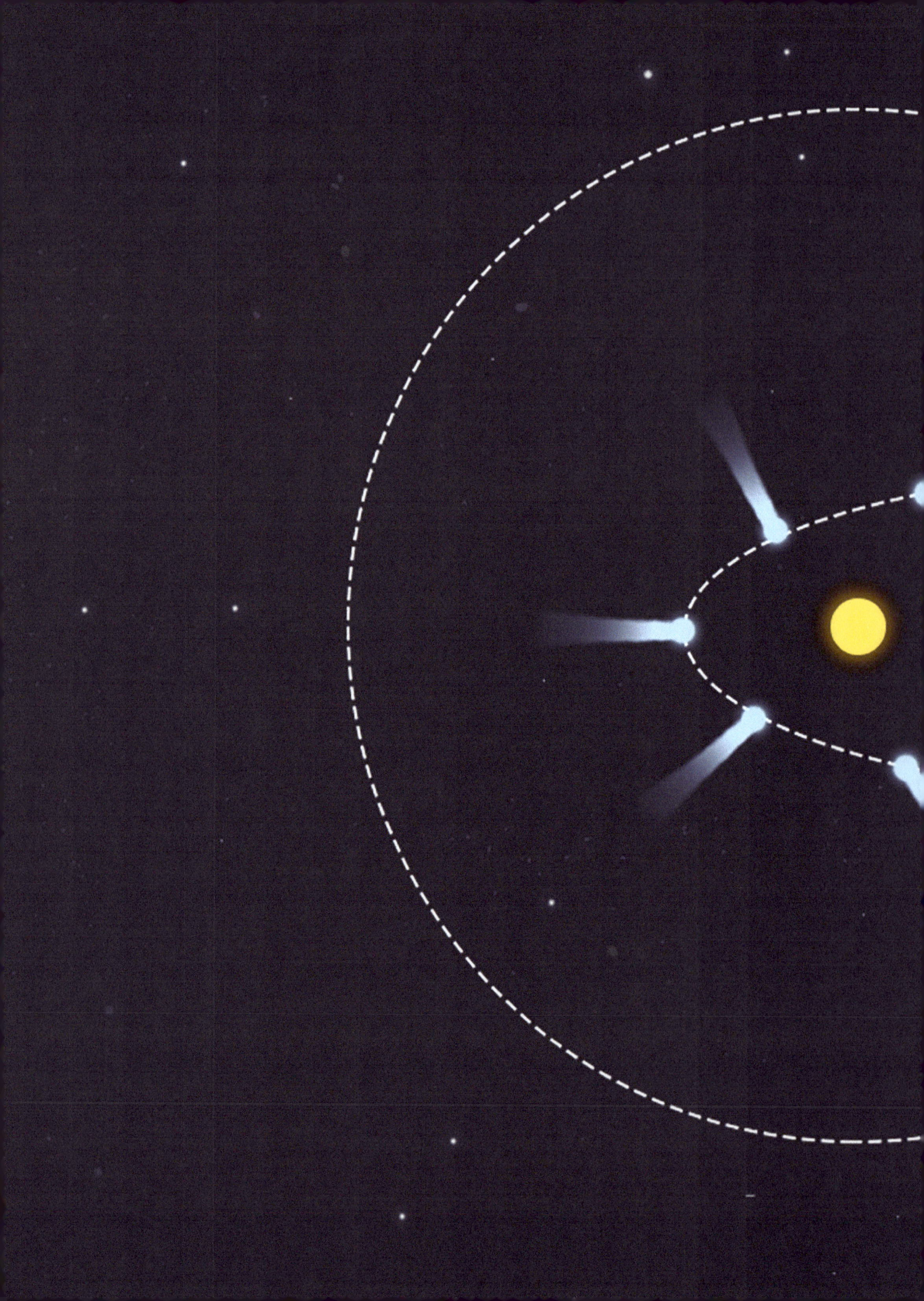

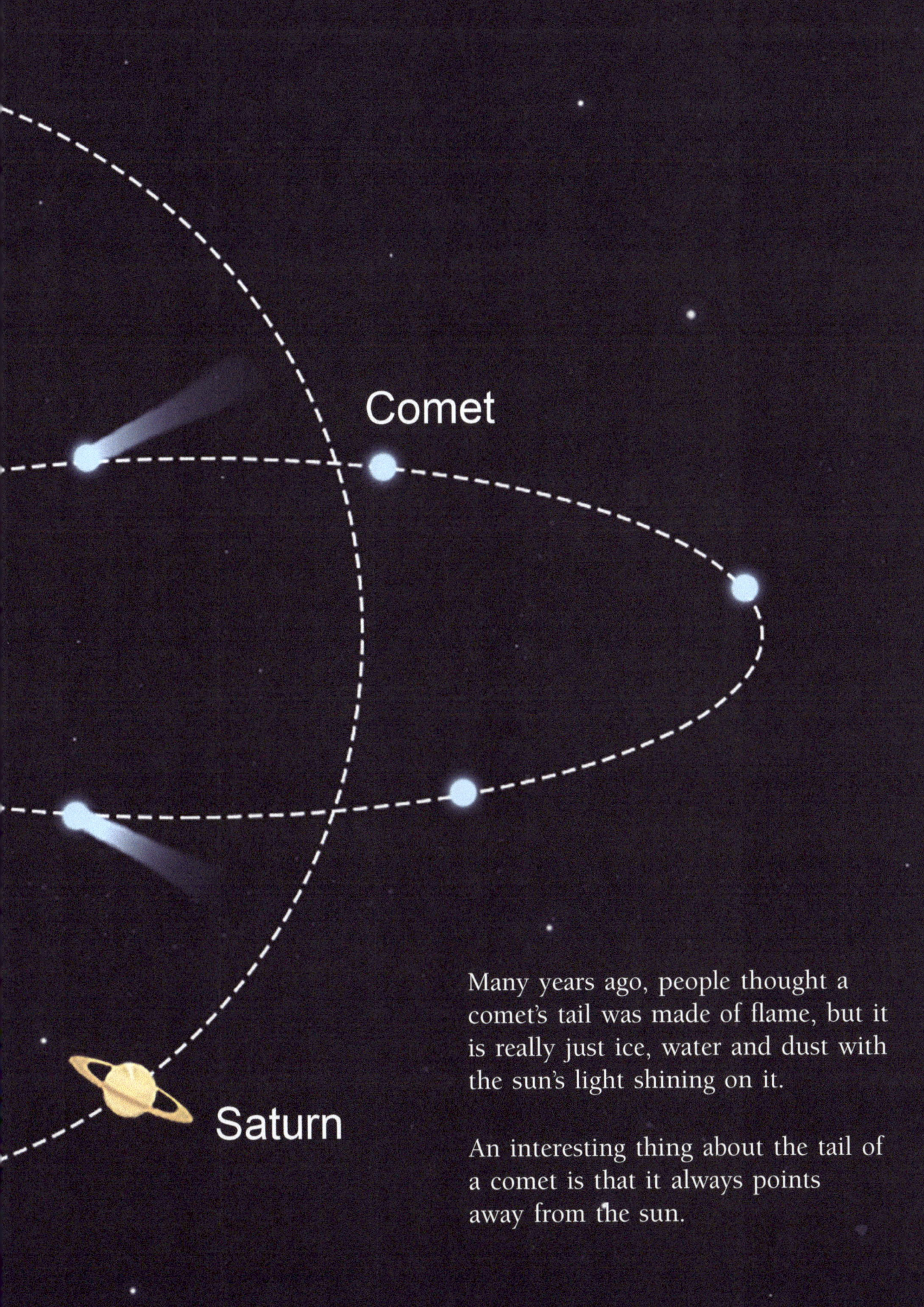

Many years ago, people thought a comet's tail was made of flame, but it is really just ice, water and dust with the sun's light shining on it.

An interesting thing about the tail of a comet is that it always points away from the sun.

COMETS

One famous comet is called Halley's Comet. This comet takes about 76 years to travel once around its orbit. It can be seen from Earth when its orbit takes it close enough.

The last time Halley's Comet came close enough to the sun to be seen from Earth was in 1986. Since then it has been following its orbit farther and farther away from the sun. In the year 2062, the comet should be close enough to see again. People watching Halley's Comet from Earth will probably be able to see it without a telescope.